Of Things
That Used To Be

Of Things That Used To Be

A Childhood on Fox Street in the
Bronx in the Early Twentieth Century

NATHAN D. LOBELL

JXJ

A publication of
JXJ Productions, Inc.

Published by
JXJ Publications
JXJPublications@gmail.com

ISBN-13: 978-0692249765
ISBN-10: 0692249761

Also available on Kindle
Book information at NathanLobell.com

Printed in the United States of America

1. Memoir. 2. Jewish History.
3. Autobiography. 4. New York History.

Book design by Tony Iatridis

CONTENTS

PREFACE 1

NOTE 11

FOX STREET IN MY DAY 13

OUR YIDDISH 15

THE PLACE 17

LIFE ON THE STREET 25

THE STREET GAMES 27

    One-a-Cat 27

    Curb Marbles 28

    Real Estate 28

    Stoopball 29

    The Common Games and The "Times" 30

STREET VISITORS 33

    The Iceman 33

    The Coal Man 34

    The Milkman 34

    The Street Cleaner 35

    The Ices Man 35

    The Merry-Go-Round 36

    The Back-Yard Musicians 37

    The Pony Picture 38

    The "I Cash" Man 38

    The Turkish Candy Man 39

The Real Food Men 40

    Nehit 40

    Knishes 40

    Pretzels 41

    Sweet Potatoes 41

    Horseradish 41

    Chewy Tar 42

    The Fruit Wagon 43

THE JANITORS 45

THE TRIBE 59

THE BLIND MAN 67

OUR ITALIANS 69

    Mr. Capelli 69

    Mr. Martello 71

MR. BRILL'S PEN 75

THE KOSHER BUTCHER 79

SOME FAMILIES 87

    The Midzhiks 87

    The Pustleblatts 88

    The Krumwegs 89

    The Hills 93

    The Szabars 95

    The Kleins 100

THE HEROES 109

    Sammy Raden 109

    Tommy Riordan 111

Al Singer 113

THE DUDS 115

Galahad 115

Nightscheh and Frood 118

The Nafkih 120

KADISCH FOR A GOY 123

LIFE IN COMMERCE 129

The Odd Jobs 129

The Laundry 129

The Florist 129

Sachet Powder 130

Jelly Apples 131

Jelly Donuts 133

The Sunday Shoot 135

Schlivovitz 135

THE WAR AND I 137

LEARNING, LEARNING, LEARNING 141

Music 141

Public (Elementary) School 148

The Tailor Shop 150

Mr. Marshall's Grocery 151

The Walk to Barretto Point 152

The Basement of the Synagogue 155

THE WAY UP AND OUT 159

PREFACE

One fall afternoon late in my father's life I was walking with him along a lane cut through the woods in Wilton, Connecticut. He started speaking: "Als Zarathustra dreissig Jahr alt war…" (When Zarathustra was thirty years old, he left his home…), the opening lines of Nietzsche's *Zarathustra*. He then remarked, "I haven't read that since I was seventeen."

Nat (as he insisted on being called in our home—he disliked "Dad," etc.) loved art, music, and making things and he was very talented at all that he did. He also loved language and literature. My name is John Joyce Lobell because he was making his way through *Finnegans Wake* for the second time when I was born. When my high school and college friends were discovering French Existentialists and advocates of a *Nouveau Roman* as rebellions against their parents, I was discovering them on my father's night table. He didn't reread Nietzsche; he didn't have to. He retained what he read, so that when I was reading Gide I could discuss books with him that he had read many years earlier. But about every five years he would dig out his old, battered, Modern Library *Jane Austen* and reread her novels. He insisted that my sister read the classics and discuss them with him, an exercise that serves her to this day in her writing.

And it was not just art, music, and literature that interested him. My father subscribed to *The Scientific American*, and to this day I recall articles I read and discussions we had in the 1950s about computers and self-replicating machines. My friends liked to hang out at our house.

Nat was one of the most educated people I have ever known, but he was also attached to his Bronx background. In one instance while he was at the Securities and Exchange Commission (SEC) he had a week of meetings with a Boston lawyer named Lewis over regulatory problems of a company Lewis was representing. When things got testy Lewis would turn on more and more of a haughty Boston accent and manner. In response, my father would become more and more Bronx in accent and manner. By the end of the week they had settled things and Lewis asked my father out to lunch. My father thought for a moment, and then decided that since everything was settled, it would be ethically all right to accept the offer. (Apparently some government officials in those days were more ethically careful than many are today.) At lunch, Lewis asked my father if his family was from Czernowitz. He said it was, and Lewis then asked what their name had been before going through Ellis Island. My father said Löbl, and Lewis replied, "I thought so. We're cousins, if distant. My branch of the family arrived in Boston rather than New York, and it quickly became apparent that it was not going to work to be Jewish in Boston, so we adopted the name Lewis." The story is interesting in several ways. The one I like is that my father could revert to his Bronxness if he wanted to.

It would have been wonderful if Nat had written about all of his life with the vividness of his depiction of his life on Fox Street, but he didn't, so, for the orientation of readers of his memoir, I will provide a very brief biographical overview.

Nat's parents came from the town of Czernowitz in the Carpathian Mountains in what was then the Austro-Hungarian Empire, and which has had several national masters since. His father came here first, and the plan was that he would make some money and send it to his wife so that she could come with the children. He neglected to send the money, so, working as a spy for several factions in the region, his wife got the money on her own to come with the children. She was apparently somewhat of a Mata Hari.

Nat was born in the Bronx on August 28, 1911, into the life you read about in this book. His visits to the Metropolitan Museum led to an interest in art, and he dropped out of high school to paint and sculpt. He shoveled coal in exchange for a basement apartment in New York's Greenwich Village and studied at the Beaux Arts Institute, the Leonardo da Vinci School of Art, and the Art Students League, among other places. He was discouraged when told that entrance into the sculptor's union, which would have assured public commissions, cost fifty dollars, an impossible amount. He had a perpetual cold while living in the chilly apartment, and when his brother, Larry, hunted him down and told him, "Mom says you can come home if you go back to high school," he accepted the offer. But for as long as I remember, Nat always had an art studio.

By the time he graduated high school we were in the midst of the Great Depression and there was little prospect of work. By then Larry had established a medical practice and he suggested that Nat move in with him and go to City College. He did, and while attending college he helped his brother with his practice and became quite medically knowledgeable.

City College was then a great educational institution, free for any New York high school graduate with qualifying grades. Nat had usually gotten As or Ds in high school depending on whether or not he was interested in the course, so his grades did not qualify, but he was admitted on the basis of an entrance exam. City College was famous for its radicalness. One of Nat's classmates had turned down a full scholarship to Harvard in order to go to City because, he said, City was better. But also because of the now famous political discussions in the cafeteria alcoves.

Job prospects were no better when Nat graduated from City and Larry suggested he go to Columbia Law School, saying he would pay for the first year and after that Nat could get a scholarship. So he did. At Columbia Nat met Griselda Holzinger, who had been born in Queens, New York, and who became his wife and my mother. After having attended Barnard College, she became one of the first women to attend Columbia Law. At Columbia, Nat became a protégé of Adolph Berle, an architect of Roosevelt's New Deal brain trust. Nat taught Berle's course when he was in Washington, and Berle got him a job in Washington on the staff of the Temporary National Economic Commission and then the Hoover Commission. He became counsel for a House committee and went on to the SEC where he rose to executive adviser to the commission, the highest position short of a presidential appointment. He wrote speeches for Presidents Roosevelt, Truman, and Johnson, but was otherwise not very political.

I was born in 1941, and my sister, also named

4

Griselda, was born in 1944. During World War II, the SEC was moved to Philadelphia to make room in Washington for war related agencies, and we lived outside of Philadelphia.

My father and mother wrote a well-received mystery novel, *The Shadow and the Blot*, published in 1949 by Harper. Griselda's father, John Holzinger (my namesake, along with Joyce), was a mystery writer. Lying in bed one night, my mother asked my father, "How would you commit a perfect murder?" My father responded. Then my mother asked, "If you were the detective, how would you solve it?" My father again responded, and my mother said, "We have to write a mystery novel."

Nat had a real affection for my mother's father, and was often at his future in-laws' house for dinner and for chess with John. When we moved to Great Neck on Long Island in 1951, my mother's parents moved in with us. Nat once described to me an illustration in a book he had as a child. It showed a family of squirrels in their cozy home, the father squirrel in his chair reading the newspaper, the mother squirrel in her chair embroidering, and the children squirrels playing with their toys on the floor. He said that when he saw that illustration, he knew it was what he wanted, and he achieved it. He made a painting of our family in our living room in Great Neck. It shows me languidly slumped in a chair petting our dog, my sister holding a cat, and my mother reading. You can see my grandparents in the next room, my grandfather reading and my grandmother clearing the dining room table. And my father showed himself seated with a drawing pad in his lap, perhaps sketching the scene.

Nat set up a studio in the basement of our home in Great Neck and made paintings and sculptures. And he painted a large abstract nude on an outer wall of the garage. I spent many wonderful hours watching him sculpt, paint, and make pottery, and made sculpture myself.

Nat was an accomplished artist. When he would sculpt a portrait bust, he would build an armature, place a large lump of clay over it, and then begin building it up with pieces of clay rolled into tapered cylinders that built the character of the subject as it built their features. Similarly in his paintings his brush strokes would build the subject's character along with their features. At one point in the 1940s when we were living outside of Philadelphia my mother suggested that he leave the SEC and set up an art supply store in the house so that he could paint full time. Nat decided against leaving the security of the law, but I think he did not regret it. He was satisfied painting for himself. He had no desire to sell his paintings.

Today Great Neck has a reputation as an affluent suburb, but at the time we lived there, many residents had come from backgrounds similar to that of my father, typically from the Bronx or Brooklyn. At the time Great Neck was strong in the arts as well as in the professions. Prominent performers and writers lived near us, and the brother of Man Ray, the Surrealist photographer, lived around the corner. He would occasionally try to sell one of Man Ray's photographs to my father for $100. Today they sell for around a million.

One of the things Nat had done while at the SEC was to draft the laws under which mutual funds work. When he left the SEC and we moved to Great Neck, he became

in-house council for a mutual fund. But he never liked
working for someone else, so he stopped working and
spent about a year looking for a small business to buy, buy
into, or start. He finally settled on a company in the South
Bronx that manufactured house-painting brushes that he
bought into with a former New Deal colleague. Due to
a change in U.S. import policies, their business strategy
soon went out the window and the company struggled.

About that period he writes, "I kept walking the
wrong way on the world's most famous one-way street
[Wall Street] and landed back in the South Bronx as
part owner of a paintbrush factory. My partner, also a
former New Dealer, and I ran that factory the way we had
run the U.S. government, as a deficit-financed welfare
institution. I soon returned to Wall Street, walked the right
way, and after some years was able to retire."

His partner had, shall we say, a colorful political past.
In 1954 when I would come home from school and watch
the Army-McCarthy hearings on television, my mother
was joining other women in her circle to bring casseroles to
my father's partner's home as a show of support. He was
in hiding and there was an FBI surveillance car parked
outside the home.

In the early 1960s Nat received a call from the owner
of a major mutual fund for which he had once worked.
The industry was under legislative attack and the leading
funds wanted him to mount a coordinated defense. He
did, leaving the paintbrush company to set up an office
in the financial district. He began the defense with a law
review article articulating his strategy and then entered
into a series of court battles. He remarked at the time, "I

have been out of the law for over a decade, but ten years ago I could not have done what I am doing now. Somehow, things had been percolating in my mind all this time."

Around the time I finished architecture school at the University of Pennsylvania, my parents moved from Great Neck to Manhattan, where Nat had an etching press in the basement. A few years later they moved to Wilton, Connecticut, in a beautiful wooded area where Nat had an entire old barn for his studio in which he not only painted, sculpted, and made etchings, but also made violas. And played music.

After my sister and I left home and my mother's parents died, Nat and Griselda had a few years alone, but then they raised my sister's kid, Michelle, and many of Nat's interests became revitalized. Michelle joined him in his studio as he painted, she read Russian novels, and she was an appreciative audience for the elaborate stories he composed in his letters to her. She became a musician, attending Yale and eventually playing the French horn in orchestras in Europe.

Wherever he was, Nat was part of a string quartet in which he played the violin and later the viola, and he often participated in amateur orchestras. And he composed string quartets. Classical music was often playing on the radio or on the phonograph in our home, and to this day when I hear certain music, memories of where I was when I first heard it come drifting back.

Nat died on August 9, 1995, just after a visit from Michelle and her baby daughter, Skye, his great grand daughter. He would be delighted with Skye's literary interests and would have enjoyed discussions with her.

My mother, Griselda, died in 2006. You can find out more about her in her book about growing up in Queens, New York, which I will publish in the future.

John Lobell
2014, New York

NOTE

Irving Howe's World of Our Fathers *grants only a few spare lines to the Bronx. The rich and colorful lives of the Jews in the Southeast Bronx where I grew up deserves a fuller description. In these pages I have tried to give a capsule account of when I was a boy there fifty to sixty years ago.*

Among other things, you will discover how to score a point at stoopball, how to cheat the gas company, and how to tamper with a butcher's scale.

You will learn how kosher meat is slaughtered, how gas is made from coal, and to prepare darrflayshe—starting with a trip to Bronx Park to gather wood and ending with a gourmet dish on a carved-out oak plank. You will find out how the buying of soup greens could be a searing experience.

The violence is here—between father and son, husband and wife. The ambitions for the children are described—for the son to be a doctor and for the daughter to marry one.

The "woikizz" or "vurrkers" (depending on what part of central Europe you came from) are overheard in the passionate arguments about the unions and their politics. The shopkeepers, their women, the peddlers, the back-yard musicians—the whole cast of characters that made up the pageant of the street is paraded in these pages.

In the streets, on the roofs, in the flats—people are everywhere—the kids and their parents struggling to find a way up and out.

Nathan Lobell
1977, Wilton

FOX STREET IN MY DAY

Often, in my grown-up life, I have dreamed of going back to Fox Street in the Southeast Bronx, the street of tenements in which I lived as a child. In my dreams Fox Street is an elegant Venetian canal lined with stately granite palazzos or is part of a city on a distant hill, a golden sunlight dappling its white marble structures. Sometimes I dream that I dig into our letterbox at 744 Fox Street and pull out an accumulation of mail, sneakers and junk that had been stored in it during the years after I left.

In this book I have gone back to Fox Street and its people and my days living in it from the years 1916 to 1926. It is, in the shimmering space of these memories, neither the place of my dreams nor what it is now in fact in the 1970s: a facade of abandoned, burned-out, crumbling tenements, an old victim (like so many live ones) of the mindless destructiveness of the last ethnic waves to wash over the place.

I will be talking mostly about Jews. But these were doublesifted Jews. They, or their parents, had the energy and will not only to escape to America from the ghettos, the hunger and the pogroms—or conscription into the Armies of Tsars and Emperors—but also to migrate from the miseries of the East Side of Manhattan into the "country," the Bronx, the Borough of the still empty lots and the clean air. They were the first wavelet of Jews who (or whose children) later moved further north into the Westchester suburbs or even exurban Connecticut, to Hollywood and to Miami. To them Yiddishkeit (the

13

state of being a Jew) was all right in its place. But they were, in vision and in aspiration, Americans; far from the Rabbi-ridden tight little ghettos of central Europe. To them it was a mark of great passage to become "ah tzititzin" (a citizen) and "zich oistzugaylen" (to yellow out, a "greener" or a "greenhorn," to integrate).

Thus, compact and relatively cohesive as the Fox Street ghetto was, it was in and part of America, porous at its borders, infusing and being infused by the larger world around it.

I dedicate this book to the people who made and shared my experiences in the little (but big enough for me) world of Fox and 156th Streets—to the older ones long since gone and to the contemporaries, even the Irish kids of the Springhurst gang, wherever they may be.

OUR YIDDISH

Since I was born as soon as possible after my mother arrived in this country to join my father, who had emigrated eight years before, my mammalooshen (mother tongue) was, literally, Yiddish. I spell it phonetically in this book as it was spoken by my family. Some readers will think it crude or merely wrong. The usual approximations of Yiddish as spelled in most books make me think that their authors' acquaintance with the language is, at best, a distant, nodding one. For example, the word for Hebrew school is "Chayder" with a strong guttural "ch" as in the German "Achtung." When I see it and other "ch" gutturals spelled with an "h" I cringe. A kid who is going to Heder, rather than Chayder, is a Jew who has slipped far from his moorings in the European ghettos. Please read all the "ch"s in this book gutturally.

Sephardic Jews, principally Spanish and Portuguese, have a lingo of their own called "Ladino." It was never heard on Fox Street. Nor was the refined German Yiddish heard. The Fox Street Yiddish was central European. Mine was of the Gahlitzeeahner variety, looked down upon by those who spoke more refined dialects. To us, if you were not a Gahlitzeeahner, you were a Litvahk. Principal differences were in articulation and vowel pronunciation. I would say "broyt'n pitter" for bread and butter. A Litvahk would say "brayt mitt pooter." And the Litvahks didn't use as many dirty words. My father's Yiddish was rich with expressive and colorful vulgarities. It borrowed as much, if not more, from the earthy language of Carpathian

15

Mountain shepherds than from the Hebrew to supplement the mongrel German of the Yiddish tongue.

Gahlitzeeahners and Litvahks both understood and disliked each other real well.

THE PLACE

If you ride into the Bronx, north on the Bruckner Boulevard overpass, after leaving the Triboro Bridge complex of roads, you will be passing numbered streets. Look left at 156th Street. Beginning several blocks off are the remains of a block-long line of red brick tenement houses, stretching from Southern Boulevard to Fox Street. These tenements, and the very few that would be within a small circle around the juncture of Fox and 156th streets, were the center of my world.

When my family first moved to 744 Fox much of the surrounding area was empty land—the "lots." It had obviously once been farmland. There were no trees, but there was some grass and there were scrubby weeds and shrubs struggling through the hard ground. The land adjoining 744 Fox had a considerable hill in the center, formed by massive rock with creviced outcroppings and dirt paths up and down its sides. One could reach the East River in a thirty to forty minute walk by going east, crossing a bridge over the New Haven railroad tracks and making a way through a wide, sparsely settled area we called Springhurst. On either side of the Springhurst expanse the land had been developed. On one side was the enormous old factory of the American Bank Note Company, dense blocks of apartment houses, and even an old convent of tan brick with a reel-tiled roof and a high-walled garden of which we could see only the tops of trees. On the other side were factories: the piano factory (whose litter included interesting scraps of

shaped wood and piano parts), pin and envelope factories, steel fabricating plants, a generating station of the
New Haven line, and so on.

But the stretch we crossed on a direct route to the
East River still contained small vegetable farms owned by
Italians whose goats were tethered near the houses, deserted barns, dark and smelling of feces, where the sun
threw thin darts of light across the debris and flies buzzed
lazily; and here and there an isolated tenement or group
of tenements, standing alone in empty, weed-filled wastes.
From them came the "Springhurst gang"—the wild and
murderous mob of Irish kids who would sometimes cross
the tracks and terrorize 156th and Fox streets.

Within a short time after we moved to Fox Street
the building began. The lots were soon heaped with
tenements—drab, tan-colored brick buildings, crushing
each other and crowding the sidewalk. It was fun while
the building was going on. Bon fires and mickey roasts
a-plenty in the still vacant land, with all the waste wood
one could want. Enough usable lumber for a "club-
house," rickety and off center; a patchwork of ill-assorted
slats, but precious to us and furnished with odd pieces
begged or filched from our apartments. Enough to build
an amphitheater in which Rosie Krumweg could produce
her memorable "show."

Square foot, by square foot, we were edged out of
the lots. From my bedroom window, where I could
once see a long view, blocks deep, I could now see only
the barren sidewall of a tenement, a narrow yard away.

We used the disappearing spaces to the last and, at
the end, had only the streets for our stickball, one-a-cat,

stoopball, and other games. We soon forgot the lots. So completely were they gone that before long I conceived the space between the Bronx and the Pacific Ocean to be miles and miles of Fox Streets, dense with tenements and teeming with people.

We had no friends in the new tenements. Their tenants were, I imagine, mostly younger, second-generation newlyweds. Within a year after these houses were occupied that part of the block was dense with baby carriages being rocked and wheeled and young women with prominent bulges and red noses carrying grocery bags. There were no, or few, kids our age in them. If there were, we would probably have spurned them as invaders or parvenus.

744 Fox was a four-story building at the corner of 156th Street. On the street level of the building were stores. The largest was Marshall's grocery at the corner to your left as you faced the stoop. Generations of kids carved their initials on the wooden sills and lintels of Marshall's windows. By my time they were already so scarred that it was hard to find a carvable space without standing on a fruit box. The next store had various owners, the one of the longest tenure being the fruit man, a short tempered red-headed man who always wore a dark cap, a grey sweater, torn at the elbows, baggy pants and a dirty white apron. Most of us kids shared common experiences with the fruit man. We would be sent for two or three or five cents worth of "zoopin greens" (soup greens) for the Friday night chicken soup. The fruit man would wrap a stalk of celery, an onion, a turnip and some parsley in a piece of newspaper. When

you got home your mother would yell, "Fahr a nickel no timmaytih? Guh back'n gaddah timmaytih." How embarrassing to have to face the fruit man again and wait while he searched for the smallest, rottenest tomato to stuff into your hand. You could still see the animus in his eyes when, the next day, you asked for a fruit box to make a pushmobile, or for your mother to sit on.

Then came the stoop, a gathering place and the place against which you knocked the rubber ball, hoping to hit a stair edge and send the ball clear across the street over your opponents' heads for a homer.

To the right of the stoop was a large store which was empty for a considerable time. For a while it was taken over by a group of activist tenants who had formed a "butcher cooperative" and was set up as a butcher store. Since my father was a butcher and, at the time, had a store on Fox Street, just a block and a half away, I was, during the heat of the cooperative fever, a social pariah. I remember appearing at the head of the stoop and looking down at a group of kids shaking their fists at me and yelling, "Butch, butch, you capitalist crook!" Fortunately, the cooperative store did not last for more than a few months. On top of the political squabbles among the members (socialists, communists, anarchists, Lovestonites and God knows what else) the employees of the store bought the cheapest grades of meat, charged high prices and stole the profits.

Next to this store was Krumweg's tailor shop. I describe it later. The last store was the candy store—which had a variety of owners, one of whom was Mr. Singer, the father of Al Singer, later the lightweight boxing champion.

The candy store was important for more than obvious reasons. Furtively, behind the counter, the owner would sell you, one for a penny, Sweet Caporal cigarettes. In front of the store was a wooden newspaper stand, around which we gathered like flies to read the headlines when the papers were delivered and, like flies were shooed away. Evenings, after the papers were gone, we were allowed to congregate at the newspaper stand. The candy-store was also a sub-station of the U.S. Mint. Part of the coinage of Fox Street was the half-cent. Deals involving the half-cent (purchase of baseball cards, settlement of bets, etc.,) were made with one two-for-a-penny caramel (thin, bitter chocolate over a chunk of sugared and hardened glue) from the candy store.

Each floor of 744, except the ground floor which contained only the janitor's apartment and the stores, had five flats. One of them was an "all-back" apartment, the one we occupied, with windows facing only the yards.

I don't think there was a single flat in the building with more than two bedrooms. But many were occupied by families with as many as six kids and some, like the Krumweg's, housed this number of kids, plus the husband of an older daughter. A bed of your own was a luxury. Until my brothers left home (one to go to college, the other to get married) I used to sleep with (and between) them in the south-facing bedroom. That bed lasted a long time. But it began to go when the room reverted to me. The first symptom was the rocking of the spring. Unless I kept myself in the mathematical center of the bed the spring tipped. Whenever I changed position it changed its slant with a bang. Several times I or my father nailed or screwed the cleats (which supported the spring) to the wooden railings of the bed. But the spring always rocked and from time to time it would drop. One of my early lovemaking sessions took place on that bed. To my timidity and anxiety was added my worry that the spring might not take our combined weights and bounces. It didn't. No sooner had we undressed and started our embraces when the spring collapsed. The session ended in ignominy for me.

After my brothers left, my sister moved in with her husband and their baby during a lean period of her husband's career (he was a travelling salesman for a pearl button factory). They took my bedroom and I slept either on a flattened Morris chair or on a cot in the combination living room and dining room—really the hegdish (disarray) room, the landing place of everything for which no other place could or would be found.

When she did it at all, my mother did the laundry in the claw legged bathtub, brought it to the south bedroom window and strung it out on a line stretched on pulleys to a pole at the far end of the backyard. It sometimes took her a week or more to do the laundry. She would leave it in the tub to soak, day after day, so that it accumulated a sickly scum and had a sour smell. The impulse to take a bath came upon me with extreme rarity. When it did, it was likely to be frustrated by the scummy laundry soaking in the tub. Showers were unknown. Sometimes my father, who was afflicted with mahreeden (hemorrhoids) would come rushing home during the day, his underclothes soaked with blood, and make for the tub. If, as happened, the tub was being occupied by the laundry, he would yell curses at my mother, fling the sopping clothes to the floor, rinse the tub and soak himself.

The bathroom served some interesting purposes. My father used it to distill schlivovitz (prune brandy). I hid there to tease my genitals and to smoke. I learned from a kid on the block to roll up toilet paper, leaving a small open space in the center, smoking the resulting cigarette. The kid, who was several years older than I and had come from Russia, explained that they used to do this in the old country to still the pangs of hunger.

LIFE ON THE STREET

Except for some sleeping, reading, eating, toilet functions, homework and music practicing there was little to keep us in our apartments. A few kids had indoor amusements: tinker-toys, erector sets, and chemistry kits. These would be used avidly for a day or so after they were bought, and then abandoned. More absorbing to those kids who had them were the tiny battery-operated crystal radio sets. You made one from a kit, mounting the exposed parts on a piece of wood. The set was operated by touching with a stiff, mounted wire various parts of a mounted piece of irregular, shiny mineral called the crystal. You probed until you could hear in your earphones, through the crackling static, something vaguely resembling speech or music. To hear anything but static was a joy. It was ecstasy if you were able to hear the call letters of a station far off. That was DX, distance, and a crystal set that could get DX was supreme in the pantheon of treasured things.

Soon came the more elaborate radios, with dials and speakers. Mrs. Bleicher, our next door neighbor, got one and, on the day of its arrival, invited my mother and me to hear it. It was, at the moment, receiving a broadcast in Yiddish. My mother stared at it and said, with wide-eyed wonder, "Sih rett Yeedish !" (It talks Yiddish!)

Television came long after my Fox Street days. But you could, if you were prescient, already notice the first nibbles at interpersonal life being made by electronics.

During the summer season even things you did normally in the apartments were done outside. On hot summer nights my father would sometimes set up a baffle he had made to cover the open well of the fire escape and I would sleep there. It was common to see kids munching a piece of bread and butter while bouncing or throwing a ball with a free hand. Many kids didn't have to climb upstairs for their snacks. I would go through the vestibule, stand at the head of the back cellar stairs and yell up at our kitchen window, "Ma! Ma!" "Voos villsteh?" (What do you want?) And I would order: bread, cake, an apple, a pickle—or money for zuzu snaps, vanilla wafers or animal crackers. Often you would see a kid seated, reading in a shady doorway. You never defecated on the street or near a building (it was different when you were on a walk across the Springhurst wastes) but an urgent piss could be taken in the cellar stairwell, under the stoop.

THE STREET GAMES

One of the most delicious of my childhood sensations was to throw off my school clothes on the last day of school before vacation time, and put a pair of fresh, stiff, new, blue overalls on my bare body. Shoes were chucked into a closet. Sneakers went on. The end of a loaf of rye or corn bread was buttered (sometimes wrapped around a scallion) and I went downstairs, stood on the stoop for a moment and drank in the delicious panorama of freedom.

Almost immediately, games were organized. The ones I describe were perennial and indigenous to the street and they persisted through the "times" (baseball cards, matchbook covers, kites, etc.).

One-a-Cat

Take a broomstick handle and cut off a bat, about three feet long. Then cut from the balance of the stick a cat, about 3 inches long. The bat is just the stick as is. The cat is sharpened at one end, somewhat like a dull pencil.

The cat is placed on the ground (the asphalt pavement), its point toward the field—the opposing players. About twenty feet down near the curb on the right side a square is marked off as a base. If there weren't enough kids to form teams the game was played by one person against all the others—from three to five. The kid at bat strikes the cat at the pointed tip—trying to make it fly up and be hit forward. If he fails in three tries he is out. If he sends the cat out he tries to run to base and home before he is tagged. Often the game would be played without foul lines. In that case a cat that was knocked into a cellar stair opening or an empty garbage pail was a sure homer. The sequence at bat was determined by the order in which, without any predetermined signal, the kids yelled: "First up... Second…" etc.

Sometimes, in one-a-cat as in other games, a kid who had just moved from another part of the city would come with different rules. Usually he would find this out to his disadvantage during a game and would grumble and sulk until he got used to our rules.

Curb Marbles

Unlike the more familiar migs, or knuckles, in which you keep all you knock out of a square, this is a wide-ranging game. Each player has a favorite "shooter"—often a large, heavy and beautiful ball bearing. You stand at the curb and shoot along it. After your shooter comes to rest your opponent tries to come within a hand span of you. If he does, he wins. You never give up your shooter. If you lose, you dig into your pocket and hand over a small, pitted glass marble. If your opponent over— or under—shoots, it's your turn to aim for his marble. And if you fail, the opportunity goes back to him. Most often the games would shuttle back and forth within about fifty to seventy-five feet from the starting point. Sometimes, if you felt adventurous, you would play the game all the way round the block to where you started. Where, in New York, could this street game be played today?

Real Estate

For this game you needed an empty lot, or an earthy stretch next to a sidewalk. You marked off a rectangle about four by five feet. You stood outside the rectangle and, holding a folding knife at the tip of an open blade, flipped it into the ground. If the blade didn't stick in you lost your turn. If it did then you scratched a line parallel with the flat of the blade from edge to edge of the rectangle. The biggest of two segments was yours. You scratched your initial in it. Your opponent stepped into his territory and tried to drive his knife into yours. If he did, he drew a line from the edge of the rectangle to your line. He obliterated the side of your line that would give him the largest patch of territory. You stood in your remainder and drove your knife back into his. This went on until one opponent had so little territory left that he could not lodge at least one foot in it.

Stoopball

This was a one-man-against-the-field game. The man "up" stood sideways at the stoop and threw the ball against the stairs. The opponents stood behind him, some all the way back beyond the opposite curb, waiting to catch the ball on the fly. If a fielder did that the thrower was out and the fielder had his turn up. If the ball bounced back on to the sidewalk in front of the stoop it was a strike—three and you were out. Similarly, if it bounced outside of a foul line chalked from curb to curb. If it bounced fair in the street before being caught it was a base. If it reached beyond the far curb and was not caught it was a homer.

The strategies were: A hard throw downward right on the step edge to send the ball as far as possible; a shallow, slanting throw to send the ball swiftly on to the pavement, low and close to the near curb; and, if you were a real expert, to try to put English on the ball, so that it would twist out of the fielder's hands.

The Common Games and The "Times"

We played the familiar games: hide and seek, Simon says, red Rover, leapfrog, etc. And word games—chalk in the first and last letters of a word and between them chalk dashes for the missing letters. Your opponent names letters at random. Each miss is an x over a dash. A guessed letter goes in. An incompleted word is a loss for your opponent. If you were smart you used words with no "e"s, as few vowels and as many unusual consonants as possible.

A mysterious clock worked in the Fox Street neighborhood. You woke up one morning and it was a "time." Among the common times was baseball cards—that came as premiums with bubble gum. You gambled with them. *A* puts down a card from his pack, facing down. *B* flips one of his cards on top. If it matches, *B* picks up the two. If not, then cards are laid down until a match occurs. As a stack rose, the pitch of excitement rose too and often would attract a circle of kids watching wide-eyed to see who would win. Sweet, sweet was the victory and bitter the loss. Kids would go far out of the neighborhood to find rare cards, not likely to be matched. The same game was played with the flap tops of matchbooks.

There would be a "kite" time, when you would see kids running down the street, or on the roofs, with one foot on the parapets, tugging at strings to coax limp kites into flight. A soaring kite at the end of your string made you feel as though you were in contact with a live thing. The urge to communicate with it led you to send "messages." You folded a piece of stiff paper into four segments and tore a bit off at the intersection of the creases. This made a hole in the center of the unfolded piece. You then made a neat tear from the edge to the hole, slipped the paper on to the kite string through this tear and watched the message make its twirling way up, up, until it reached the kite. We never understood the aerodynamics of this phenomenon. But we knew it worked.

As kite time ebbed you would see kite corpses, their tails (torn bed sheets mostly) hanging sadly from street lamps, poles and wires, or dangling from a projecting wall ornament.

Punchboard time was feverish. The board was about three inches by five inches with about forty or fifty holes plugged with small, rolled up slips of paper. At the top on one side was a big hole. You had a "pusher," a metal rod that could push out the small slips. Your victim could choose his stakes—from a nickel to a quarter a push. Some of the pushed out slips, a very few, would award a modest multiple of the cost of the push. Most were duds. One of the small slips entitled the player to expose the grand prize—a somewhat larger multiple of the cost of the push. The boards could be gotten at Cheap Alberts—a store on Westchester Avenue under the El that sold a fascinating array of junk: noise makers, masks, tricks, rubber spiders, true-to-life turds, etc. Sometimes we would take the long walk to Cheap Alberts just for the fun of looking through the window.

I once bought a board—very reasonable—and stood

outside of Marshall's grocery on the corner waiting for victims. They came. My board was soon pushed out. And although I was obligated to pay off the grand prize should it have been won early, I was able to pay off from my revenues and have a handsome profit left.

My first board was my last. I felt ashamed. It was too easy. People were too gullible. You could see the lust in their eyes when they took the pusher in hand and their bitterness when they pushed out a dud. But they paid and pushed compulsively. Some kids with boards spent their money pushing at other kids' boards. I never did.

Who declared that a Time had come? What determined the coming of a Time? Nobody ever knew. We responded like a herd to a basic and shared impulse, knowing that we had to, but not why.

STREET VISITORS

An essential and colorful part of the life of Fox Street was provided by the commerce that came through—on foot or on horse and wagon mostly; only rarely by truck.

The Iceman

He clip-clopped his horse to the front of the building and with his tongs reached in and pulled a block of ice toward the back ledge of the wagon. He scored the block with a point of his tongs, and with a pick made several stabs along the scored groove, separating off a piece neatly. With his tongs he flung the ice on his shoulder, which was covered with a rubber mat. He trudged up the stoop and into the building, leaving a fine trail of droplets behind him. He knew the size of every ice block for every customer—ranging from a fifteen to a thirty-five cent piece. He would open the top door of the double-tiered icebox, shove the remnant of the last piece aside and fling in the fresh block. You paid him then and there. Water from melted ice collected in a flat metal pan under the box. If you forgot to pull out and empty the pan (my chore) you would soon see a puddle on the floor around the box.

There were several reasons for interest in the iceman. His wagon was dark and cool. It had an unforgettable smell of wet wood and burlap. Besides, it was the source of a goodie. When the iceman was in the building, delivering, we would climb into the wagon and pick pieces of ice and scraps to suck and chew. It was a brave thing to do. One:

you might get caught by the iceman. His curses in loud and Slurvian Italian were awesome. Two: your mother might catch you and slap the ice away. Three: you ran the risk of serious disease. We kids had a theory that since ice was made with *am*monia, sucking it might give you *pneu*monia. It was plausible to us; but we dared.

The Coal Man

Among the earliest motor trucks coming to the neighborhood were those driven by the coal men. Some buildings were so arranged that the coal man would run a chute from the back of his truck into the cellar. He would raise the front of the truck and the coal would come tumbling down the chute. If I remember right he used to stand at the rear of the truck with his hand on a lever. He would watch the coal spilling down and at a certain point would pull the lever, stopping the flow. Did he estimate the tonnage by eye? In other buildings the coal was delivered in hoppers made of heavy, wood-reinforced canvas. The men would dump the coal into the street, shovel it into these hoppers, hoist the hoppers on to their shoulders and plod in and out of the building.

The Milkman

Few people in our row of buildings used delivered bottle milk. We had ours ladled into our milk pails at Mr. Marshall's. He would pry off the cover of a large pail, plunge in his long, flat-bottomed dipper, stir the milk and ladle out a quart at a time. The milk would be cool and bubbly in your pail.

The milkman with the wagon did a good business in the newer buildings. You would see him only rarely—

mostly in early mornings of mid-summer when you left your apartment to escape the stale, hot, damp air inside. Often the milkman's horse or a furtive cat were the only moving things on the block. Then you walked over to watch. The milkman was a hustler in a white cap and jacket. He would eye you suspiciously while flinging the cold bottles into compartments of a metal carrying tray or juggling empty bottles into the tray. Meanwhile his horse, big, patient, fragrant with the smell that nothing on earth but a horse has, would stand, switching at flies with its tail, or dropping a heavy, steaming load of dung.

The Street Cleaner

This gentleman, always Italian, would come pushing a large, metal drum on wheels and wielding a push broom with stiff brown bristles. He would walk leisurely along the curb, pushing his broom until he collected a pile of dust, dung, paper scraps and old rags. Then he would pull a flat scoop shovel from his little wagon and shovel the debris into the metal drum. In his slow patient way he would move on until we were tired of watching him. Sometimes, however, he would bend to pick up and examine an object. When he did we rushed to see what he had found. He never told us or showed us. He was a non-communicator.

Other visitors were intermittent. They always came as a welcome surprise and always gave us something wonderful to watch or to do.

The Ices Man

The ices man had a small flat pushcart bearing a burlap-covered block of ice. Running the length of the cart was a tray of bottles with colored and flavored liquids. These had pointed nozzles. For a small amount (2¢, 3¢) he would scrape the ice block with a cuplike scraper having a toothed bottom. The scrapings would rise in the cup and be dumped into a cone-shaped paper holder. You called out your color, or flavor, and he would shake some of the liquid out of a bottle on to the scrapings. Even though he invariably chose a shady spot in which to park and you tended to eat your ices near his cart it was not long before the cold shavings merged with the colored liquid and went down as a drink. Such is the power of legitimacy that we never paused to wonder why ice from the iceman's wagon might give you pneumonia, but ice from the ices man's wagon would not.

The Merry-Go-Round

If we had visits from organ grinders I cannot recall any but one—with a small, red-capped monkey on a long chain. The little thing had pink-rimmed and pathetic eyes, grasped its tin cup in tiny hands and darted about nervously. It was sadder than the music. But the musical merry-go-round was a frequent visitor. This was a horse-drawn flat cart carrying a merry-go-round with a few frantic looking, paint-peeling horses and a pointed, multi-colored roof. Around the center were small benches for the very young or very timid. The horses did not rise and fall. You paid your few cents, mounted a step through an open gate and ran to your horse. Then you waited, and waited. It seemed forever. But it was not until the merry-go-round man had filled the wagon, or was sure there were no more customers, that the turning began. The gate would close, the man would give the merry-go-round a push with his hand and then grind you around by turning a large wheel (obviously geared underneath to the merry-go-round platform). The music played, clanging, raucous and out of tune, with many missing notes. But it was music to us. You banged your behind up and down on the horse to simulate an exciting ride. Almost, it seemed, as soon as you had started, the turning stopped, the gate opened and you were shoved off to make room for the next batch of waiting kids.

The Back-Yard Musicians

Suddenly you would hear, from the airshaft, a beery voice singing *I'm forever blowing bubbles, Pretty bubbles in the air; They fly so high, Nearly reach the sky, Then like my dream, They fade and die...* It was a back-yard troubadour who bowed hat in hand when he had finished and waited for the coins to come down. Some considerate people wrapped their coins in twists of newspaper. Others merely tossed them, bouncing, on the pavement.

Or you would hear a scratch violin sobbing out "Moonlight and Roses" or "Humoresque" or a then popular Yiddish ballad, "Ich Bin a Boarder bei mein Weib..." the tale of the clever man who, observing how much better than he the boarder was treated, left home and moved back as a boarder. Or "Dee greene cuzzeene" (the greenhorn cousin).

Sometimes it would be a clarinet, most likely playing klezmer (working, low class, for hire) music such as a "fraylach," the kind of wild, whirling music to which the "kazatzkee" (the Cossack kneeling and leg-kicking dance) was danced at weddings. Or a saxophone sobbing out a popular hit like "Lena" (is the queen of Palestine) or "Oh, Katharina" (*to keep my love you must be leaner... Learn to swim. Join the gym.* And... believe it or not—*eat farina...*)

The Pony Picture

Somewhere between the service street people (the umbrella repair man, the knife grinder, the pot mender) and the amusements was the man with the camera and the pony. You ran upstairs, begged a quarter from your mother and fidgeted until your turn came to sit on the pony and be photographed. You sat still, smiled at the command and watched, bewitched, as the man's head disappeared under the black cloth hanging at the back of his camera and he fiddled with the cap over the lens. Then he appeared again, got you down from the pony, and while you watched, pulled the slide from somewhere in the camera, yanked out the oblong piece of tin, dipped it into a cup of liquid suspended under the camera, fished it out, slapped it into a cardboard frame and handed you yourself gawking at the lens, head down. Upstairs you ran, unable to take your eyes from it. When the man was through he snapped together the legs of his wooden tripod, hoisted it to his shoulder and led his pony down a way, where he would set himself up again.

The "I Cash" Man

From time to time you would hear, coming from the back yard, the cry, "Ole cloes... I cash cloes... ole cloes... I

38

cash cloes." And you would see a man with a big stuffed sack, jingling coins in his pocket, looking up and around, repeating his call. If you beckoned him, you would give him your apartment number. He would soon appear and, if you didn't have your clothes ready, would stand with hand on hip, waiting with the air of one whose precious time you were wasting. Whatever you brought out he would eye with contempt, as though you were insulting him. He would lift his pack and make a move toward the door. If you didn't stop him first with a "Noo?" he would pause and say, wearily, "So ahm upstehs awready, a qvudder fah de lot." If you gathered the clothes to take them back he would stretch a hand to you. "Zaytach! (look you) I em a poor men. I hef to mek a leeving. Varriyi tink I'm gadding fo a soot—efter I'm boining alt de eyes to fix it. So vat can I affudder?" He softened you and made you feel guilty if you insisted on fifty cents for a perfectly good, outgrown boy's suit.

The Turkish Candy Man

Except for a fat, shiny-faced man who came around with a tray of Turkish candies, most of the food vendors sold nourishment rather than sweets. The Turkish candy tray had three kinds of goodies. One was a sesame candy, obviously made from a syrupy preparation, poured onto waxed paper and allowed to harden. Then strips were cut in it and diagonal cuts made across the strips, so that the piece you bought was diamond shaped. This was my favorite. Another candy on his tray was chunks of hard but chewy nougat, pink white and light blue, with pieces of almond in them. Another was a frosted candy

39

(Turkish delight) like hardened gelatin, which it probably was, dusted with confectioner's sugar.

Everything on that tray stuck to your teeth. I lost at least three "first" teeth on Turkish candy.

While I am on the subject of teeth let me tell you about Dr. Bach, the local dentist. I had more cavities than teeth and was a frequent occupant of his chair. Invariably, after a quick poke of his mirror around my mouth he would shake his head sadly and warn me against sweets. And always as I left he gave me a lollipop.

The Real Food Men

A variety of ready-to-eat food vendors would come to the block.

Nehit: Nehit came in a large porcelainized metal pot pushed on baby carriage wheels and somehow kept hot. It contained boiled chickpeas, known in Yiddish as "arbisslahch" or "nehit," which, I believe is an Arabic word. I was constantly discovering Yiddish words imported from languages other than German, English or Hebrew. For example "pantufflin" slippers) and serviettle (napkin) from the French. Roumanian, Polish and Russian phrases were used wholesale by my father, usually prefaced with "Der goy zoogt a vertle..." (The peasant has a saying...).

The nehit was spooned on to a paper dish and before being handed to you was liberally sprinkled with salt and pepper.

Knishes: These were of two kinds, both sold hot. One was potatoes and onion, highly spiced, wrapped in flaky dough, wound into a coil and baked. The other knish was the same mixture, flattened into a patty, breaded and deep fried. Each kind had its partisans. As far as I remember the same man never sold both.

Pretzels: While pretzel vendors were normally sedentary, sitting at busy places with their basket on a box, they sometimes came through Fox Street. The pretzels were shiny in those days, big, fat, underbaked, with their fat tops heavily crusted with black poppy seeds and large salt crystals. They were rubbery. They fought you back. But they were good. If you were superhygienic you refused to take one from the stock racked up on sticks set around the basket. You made the man lift up the white cloth and pull one out from underneath.

Sweet Potatoes: Sometimes a man came through pushing a vehicle that looked like a sheet metal chest of drawers with a bottom tray of glowing coals. It was the sweet potato man. When you came up he would ask, "Fahd hah mahtsh?" You would say, "two cents," "three cents," or "a nickel." He would open drawers, searching for a potato of the appropriate size at the price, and give it to you wrapped in a square of newspaper. His difficulty was mostly in finding one small enough at your price. Sometimes he would cross-examine you about how much money you had or asked to see the money in your hand. If he had to, he would grumblingly cut a piece from a whole potato.

Horseradish: I have not, since those days, seen another variety of sedentary vendor I watched with as great an interest as I watched the horseradish grinder. This was invariably a little old man or lady sitting at the curb on a busy shopping day. Set on a wheeled box was a little grinding machine. The machine had a perforated drum with

41

sharp projections at each perforation and was turned by a crank. The horseradish (a long white root) was pushed against the turning wheel and the shredded grindings, wet and fragrant with the characteristic sharp smell of horseradish, would collect and be poured into a small bottle.

Few Jews would eat their boiled beef (they rarely prepared it any other way) without a generous scoop of horseradish on the dish. Horseradish or "chrayn" came in two ways: plain white and purplish red. The red was made simply by adding beet juice. Horseradish spoiled very quickly, becoming discolored and tasting merely sour and rotten. So you bought small amounts and, when you bought from the little old grinder, you were sure you were getting it fresh.

Chewy Tar: Involuntary purveyors of an oral goodie were the men who came around to repair potholes in the street. They used two materials. One was coarse asphalt. This was dumped into the hole and smoothed over with heavy push irons on long handles. The irons were kept hot at a forced blower stove. In a drum over that stove was the *real* stuff. This was a shiny, smooth pitch, kept hot and viscous. When the hole was filled and smoothed this shiny stuff was ladled out and poured as a seal neatly around the edge of the repair. This crew always fascinated us. The smell was strong and pleasant. The forced flame made a steady roar, except when it began to flutter. Then a man would rush up and pump a compressor handle to revive the flame. And, most of all, the men would let you pick drippings of the shiny tar from the edge of the drum. This had a pleasant piney taste, a wonderful consistency, and was reputed to be the best tooth whitener you could get.

It had another use. One Saturday morning (while his butcher store was closed) my father walked to one of these drums and dug out a lump of tar. While I watched he modeled a stag—legs and horns and all. I thought it was beautiful. When it was done he tossed it back into the drum.

The Fruit Wagon: At times when the store south of the stoop at 744 Fox was empty (or not occupied as a fruit and vegetable store), the fruit wagon would stop in front of the building. It came down the block, rattle-rattle, the fruit man leading his horse, bawling out "Pitrayriss," "Binnenniss," "Owniawns," and repeating his call. If a customer called from a window on the block he would stop and wait for her to come down. His boxes were sloped so that you could see the merchandise, and prices were posted on large brown bags (apparently lettered with a cotton-tipped shoe polish dipper) draped over sticks. Often he would rest his horse in front of our building, fill a pail of water for it at Marshall's grocery, or put on its feedbag. We would watch the animal snuffle its way through the oats and, at the bottom of the bag, toss it to get the grain into its mouth.

Sometimes the fruit wagon man ran a fruit store, which would be tended by his wife while he led the horse around. The father of one of my early girlfriends had such a store. The store and the wagon kept them in a comfortable well-furnished apartment, paid for expensive piano lessons for their daughter and, eventually, sent her to Barnard College.

THE JANITORS

For some reason, janitors, or their daughters, or both, stand out very clearly in my memory during and even before the Fox Street era of my life. I was born on the ground floor of a tenement in the Bronx named Washington Avenue within a year after my mother came to this country. One of the memories of this place begins the chain of recollection of janitors and their daughters.

The janitor of Washington Avenue lived in a ground floor apartment next to ours. The lady janitor was a fat woman with two daughters. The older was chubby, with long hair. The younger was my age—about three at the time of my keenest recollections of her.

The older daughter had the longest hair of any person I have ever seen. It was thick, full and hung down to her heels. The combing of this hair by her mother was a daily ritual and everyone within blocks knew when it was taking place—because of the noise. The janitor's apartment like many others had a built-in wall mirror, ceiling to floor. It was flanked by wooden pillars, had a box-like base and a carved crest.

Sometimes when I was playing with the younger child I would watch the daily combing ritual. The older girl would be caught, after a chase, and pushed to face the mirror. Her mother sat behind her, wielding a very long, heavy comb. While the mother pulled at the hanks, scalp to ends, the girl held her hands clasped at her side, her eyes tightly shut, and screamed. This was no ordinary scream. It was high, loud, piercing and unrelenting. You would listen, bothered or fascinated, or both, waiting for seemingly interminable screams to rise to a penultimate high and piercing note and to end. You were sure that the next scream must be weaker. Not so. It came, with that same incredible length and intensity, to be broken only by a bang on the ear from the comb.

The younger daughter was the cause of my first awe and envy. She was short, thin, curly haired and bright and I marveled at her abilities. She was often sent on errands about the tenement and was trusted with the janitor's keys. These hung from a very large ring, were of assorted sizes and shapes, and made an impressive jingle. I remember watching her once as she came up the vestibule, jingling the keys. When she reached her door she jerked the key ring and, with an unerring pinch, picked one out, stood on her toes, put the key into the lock, twisted and *voila*, pushed her door open. My feeling about that was matched later in life by nothing less than Ruggiero Ricci's prestidgitary performance of Paganini's violin impossibilities.

At 744 Fox Street, when we moved there and for about four or five years after, the janitor work was done by the Solovickis. They were a Polish couple with a daughter about my age. Mr. Solovicki was a well-built man with sandy hair and a generous red mustache that ended in curls twisted almost up to his eyes. Mrs. Solovicki was small, wiry, bandy-legged. Whatever Mr. Solovicki did (which wasn't much besides drink, tend the cellar coal furnace and collect the garbage) he did with panache. I loved to watch him and—perhaps—for that reason he allowed me to follow him during his chores. There was a big and pleasant rhythm to the way he scooped coal into his large shovel and flung it through the open furnace door on to the mound of glowing and shimmering coals inside. The furnace room was dark and the red light of the glowing coals would paint wonderful shapes on his arms and face.

Heat, when it came, was given by steam radiators, one or two in each apartment—never in a bedroom. On cold nights the steam made a pleasant, hissing noise as it came out of the shiny valves screwed into the side of the radiator. There wasn't always heat. And often an irate tenant would bang on the radiator to demand it. Then another would start banging. Then others, until the whole building rang. I imagine that if the ethnic background of the tenantry were not predominantly Jewish, the banging would have assumed a collective rhythm. It did not, and the result was a steady, undulating clamor.

The garbage was collected at about seven p.m. Running the height of the building was the dumbwaiter shaft, with a waist-high door in the hall on each floor. The dumbwaiter was a two-tiered wooden box hoisted by a thick rope riding on a pulley at the top of the shaft. At collecting time Mr. Solovicki would go down to a cellar room onto which the dumbwaiter shaft opened. He would stick his head into the shaft, look up and yell. "Gah-bitch! Gah-bitch!" Then, from every apartment, the women and (or) kids would stream out with the pails or the bags and stand in line at the dumbwaiter door. If you lived (as we did) on the second floor or below it was important to be first on line. Mr. Solovicki started at the top floor and worked his way down, expertly stopping the dumbwaiter flush with the doors. If the shelves were too crowded to take your garbage you asked him to lower the dumbwaiter a little to see if there was room on the top—despite Mr. Solovicki's frequent yell of "Naw gahbitch on the top, plizz!" If not, you yelled, "All full." Mr. Solovicki would then drop the dumbwaiter, empty the pails or dump the bags into metal trashcans and you had to wait until he raised the dumbwaiter again.

The trashcans were stored in the cellar room until the next morning. Then Mr. Solovicki carried them up the cellar steps to the street level, flung them deftly over the low iron fence that bordered the cellar stair well and line them up, to wait for the city collection. Invariably the cats would crawl out from God-knows where and leap on top of the pails which were, most of the time, coverless. Then Mrs. Solovicki, whose window was right above the cellar stair well, would throw her window up and fling a pail of water on the cats. No one I knew had a cat for a pet—although some had dogs. Never a large dog. These were for the garages on Southern Boulevard and for Springhurst people. The neighborhood pets were divided into two kinds, regardless of pedigree: all small, ratty smooth-haired dogs were fox terriers; and all small, white fluffy dogs were poodles.

My father once brought home a "poodle," a frightened, nervous, little creature that ran about wildly, whined and would not be comforted. My mother screamed that she did not want a dog in the house and demanded that it be thrown out at once. She compromised. "Noo den, morgen in der free." We found the poor thing the next morning lying under the kitchen table on its back, its legs stuck up stiffly—dead.

Mr. Solovicki separated newspapers and magazines from the rest of the trash. These he piled in a deep window well in the garbage room in the front wall of the building. The platform of the outside cellar stairs above this window was perforated and let some light sift through. I would often go down to the garbage room and pore through these newspapers and magazines, not bothered by the sour smell that permeated the place. As to the flies—they were as commonplace to us as the air we breathed. To this day I remember vividly an article in the Sunday Supplement to the "American," a then popular newspaper.

It was headed, "The Dangers of Kissing: Is Amorous Osculation a Transmitter of Disease?" I understood the headline, despite the fact that the word "osculation" was new to me. It had an inviting, pornographic sound. The article was illustrated with a schematic drawing of a mustached man in profile, his lips meeting those of a profiled female. A small, vicious looking bacterium (like a miniature crab) was shown moving from the mustache toward the woman. I may have been impressed then, but I have been an addicted osculator all my life.

Mrs. Solovicki's main function was cleaning. Other functions—such as repairs and maintenance—you did yourself if you didn't want to plotz (collapse) waiting for Mr. Solovicki. Daily Mrs. Solovicki would carry her big sweeping broom to the top floor and sweep halls and stairs, raising an increasing flurry of dust and scraps, until she ended at the foot of the stoop, whence the dirt was swept into the gutter.

Once a week Mrs. Solovicki, with her rolling, bandy-legged walk, and her thin sinewy arms, lugged a large pail of soapy water, a brush and a hank of rags, grey-dirty, up to the top floor. On her hands and knees she scrubbed and wiped halls and steps, down to and including the vestibule and stoop. If you had to pass her while she was scrubbing she would move aside and without looking up utter a malediction in low, guttural Polish.

The vestibule was short and narrow. In a small space directly beyond the entrance were the mailboxes (no push bells). Beyond, to the right, was the door of the janitor's apartment (the only one on the ground floor). Beyond that door, on the right, rose the steps to the upper floors. To the left, beyond the steps, at the end of the vestibule, was a metal door, opening on the wooden platform of the stairway leading down to the pavement of the yard, or airshaft. You reached this metal door by going down two steps and walking forward a few feet. Under the rising hall stairs was a comfortable little nook, often used in hide-and-seek.

Mostly, of course, the little girls played by themselves; jacks, jump rope, or bounce ball, slapping the ball down, one hand, two hand, one leg over or both legs over in turn. They chanted:

Baker, bake bake a cake
Send it up to forty-eight…

or

I spied Mistress Mary

Sitting on a bumble airy
Just like you!

or

Old man Kelly
Had a pimple on his belly
And his wife cut if off
And it tasted just like jelly.

Sometimes they asked to join the boys' games. It was rarely allowed. Most of the boy-girl fraternizing was between single pairs, and, while it began innocently in playing "house" it often ended in the altered relation of physician and patient.

When we were eight or so, a friend came to visit the Solovicki girl. She was a schoolmate from the parochial school. This child wore prim, grey clothing, was always neatly dressed, her short, mouse-colored hair perfectly combed. She was slender, had a pinched little Irish face and was quiet and demure, sitting mostly by herself and making colored-thread cross-stitches on doilies. Every apartment I saw that had a girl in it was blotched with these doilies; round, square, scalloped, plain; on bureaus, tables, and chests of drawers.

This girl was my first "crush." I tried every way I knew to interest her. To no avail. She sat and sewed. Sometimes she would look sideways at me, with a small curl in her lip. I suspected that she was contemptuous of me as a little "sheeny," but I didn't care. The Solovicki girl ended the matter by saying: "Leave her alone. She's going to be a nun."

For a time the janitor work in the adjoining building on 156th was done by a Polish family with a horde of children. One of them was a tow-headed girl my age. The janitor's apartment in this building was in the cellar.

One day this family moved. I was one of the kids on the block watching the furniture being brought up from the cellar. A large bedspring was carried up. It was dropped at one end to lean it against the cellar well railing. When it dropped, a veritable rain of bed bugs fell to the ground. There was a thick border of the small, brown scampering things all around the spring. We stamped and shuffled but made little progress against the scattering beasts that fled in all directions. I had a sudden vision of the kind of life these people led.

The most interesting janitor I knew was Mr. Bassett. He was a single man who followed the Solovickis at 744 Fox Street. He was tall, with very long arms and enormous hands. He was slow moving and very gentle. I call him Mr. Bassett because he had a very long, sad face with small round eyes, a long fleshy nose and a jowled chin with fatty nodules—not equally placed—on each side.

Our first experience with Mr. Bassett was this: On the first Friday evening of his tenure as janitor he knocked at the door, bowed slightly and said, in atrocious Yiddish, as he came in, "Ick bin the shahbiss goy."

Then he went to the gas stove, reached a match from the little tin box into which you stuffed the cardboard match box so that the matches fell into a curved receptacle at the bottom, and lit a small flame on each of the burners. We watched him, wide-eyed. Then I explained that this wouldn't be necessary, we took care of it ourselves. Mr. Basset must have served previously in a place where religious Jews (not allowed, among other labors, to light a fire on the Sabbath which begins at sundown on Friday) used him for this chore. A gentile so used is called a "shahbiss goy."

There is a Jewish joke about this: On a train in Central Europe two Jews meet and talk.

"Where do you come from?"

"Cholodetz."

"A big city?"

"No. A small place."

"Are there many goyim in Cholodetz?"

"A few. And you, where do you come from?"

"Moscow."

"How many goy in Moscow?"

"Thousands upon thousands!"

"What? What for do you need so many goyim?"

To get back to the subject of gas, let me explain that we lit and cooked with gas. In the beginning, our light came from a fanshaped flame jetting out of a metal tip on the gas fixture. Then we progressed to the gas mantle—a small hood of extremely fragile woven material set on a ceramic ring and clamped into the fixture. This hood would give a strong light. But the mantle, which came in a small red box, was so fragile that if you touched the hood when removing it from the box or when applying a match, it would shatter into a fine powder. After some use it would disintegrate by itself and a shapeless flame would come out of the fixture.

Each apartment had a gas meter. They were "quarter" meters. To get a supply of gas you would stand on a chair and push a quarter into a slot in the meter. Periodically a collector came around, opened the meter with a key and emptied the coin-box. If you saw the light flame begin to dim or the stove jets die down and had no quarter on hand you were in trouble—unless you knew some of the tricks. One of the tricks was to bang the meter several times with a stick. This was good for a two or three hour supply of gas. Another, devised by my oldest brother, was much better. You pushed into the slot a long metal wafer as thick and as wide as a quarter. It had to be long enough to go all the way into the slot and project out a bit. You kept the metal piece pressed against the inside of the slot by stretching a piece of tape over its protruding end and fastening the tape to the meter box. This gave you gas for a long time. My mother was perennially worried about being caught by a collector. Not my father. "Ahz mih chahpt mirr kennen zay mirr reef en pisher." (If I'm caught they can call me pisser; i.e. to hell with them.) Nobody had to call my father pisher. We knew just about when to expect the collector.

The gas we used was made locally from coal and stored in the enormous round tanks that are familiar to-day but now house natural gas, piped from thousands of miles away. I would sometimes walk down to the Hunts Point area near the East River, where the gas was made. In the lowering evening it was a thrilling sight. A row of high, narrow ovens (in effect compartments of a single long steel box) was loaded with coal from a moving hopper that ran in a rail along the top. When each box was filled the top flap would close and the coal would be heated by a bank of flames underneath the ovens. After a while the steel box began to glow. When the cooking was done and the hot gas piped off the ovens, a steel pusher, about the size of the narrow side of the ovens, moving on rails in front of the ovens, would go from oven to oven, push at the front and propel a solid, orange mass of gleaming coke, with a blue, hot aura around it, into an empty steel railroad car at the back of the ovens. The sky would be lit by the crumbling mass as it was pushed out, a blast of heat would come at you and the mass would tumble into the car with a shattering roar and a shower of sparks.

To complete the story of Mr. Bassett I have to tell you about the 156th Street side of our building. Directly beyond Mr. Marshall's grocery store window on 156th was a raised platform of iron slats, bordered at the back by the brick wall of the building and on the sides by iron rails projecting from the wall. Directly above this platform was the fire-escape ladder which lay horizontal when not used and which sloped down from the lowest tier of the fire escapes above if you stepped on a top rung. The purpose of the platform was to serve as a landing for that ladder when it was dropped.

However, the platform had a more important use. Except for early morning when the sun rose directly on a line with 156th street, that platform was in the shade. So, on a hot summer day, it was a favorite gathering place for as many kids as could huddle on or about it. It was a place for discussing the merits of baseball players, Frank Merriwell, the latest exploits of Doug Fairbanks or western heroes (Tom Mix, Hoot Gibson) or vying with each other in disgust with "sissy movies" (slick hair, coat tails, bow ties and kisses in the garden). It was where jokes and riddles were swapped. "Don't drink Arbuckle coffee. Why? It lays heavy on the stomach." (This was topical; it referred to the then current Hollywood scandal about Virginia Rappe and the comedian Fatty Arbuckle. At a wild Hollywood party Mr. Arbuckle and Miss Rappe were off together. During intercourse her insides were injured. She hemorrhaged and later died.) "When is a pig not a pig? When it turns into a sty."

Sometimes a mischievous kid (usually Muttie Krumweg) would empty a pail of water on an upper fire escape so that the drippings would fall on our heads. Sometimes we would tie a stone to a rope, fling it up to catch a rung of the horizontal ladder above us, pull it down and clamber on it, playing lookout on the mast of a pirate ship.

When Mr. Bassett caught us at it he would admonish us in the sternest manner he could command, which, compared with the bawling of Mr. Solovicki or the high pitched yammering of Mrs. Solovicki, was gentle enough.

Once in awhile when we were huddled on the platform we discussed music. "Do you take from Mr. Sentner?" "Isn't he terrible!" "Where are you in the book?" "What piece did he give you?"

Mr. Bassett came by while we were having one of these discussions and he stopped to listen. "Do you like music?" he asked.

"Well, yeah; sort of"; "Sometimes"; "I guess!"

"Wait here," he said and disappeared. A short time later he came back with a cello, a bow and a fruit box. He sat and played. He made atrocious sounds. But his head was back, his eyes closed, his face suffused with ecstasy. When he was done he stood up, shook his head sadly. "I am an inveteran musician," he said, and added, "If I only had a chance! Practice! Practice!"

THE TRIBE

Except for the Chevreh Mishnaies (companions of the law) to whom I listened from a distance in the basement of the shoal (Synagogue) my experience with the old Jews who wore long black coats, round-topped hats with brims, beards and long payiss (sideburns) was not good.

You would hear a knock on your apartment door. When you opened, one of the tribe would push his way in and, without a word, fish a hammer and nail from somewhere in his cloaking, drive the nail into a door trim and hang on it a blue box with a metal top slotted to receive coins. The box had on it a blurred and indistinct picture of a building with figures of some kind lustered in the foreground. He would explain in brusque and rapid Yiddish that this Pushkeh (box) was for nedoovehs (alms) for an orphanage or moyshev zikaynem (old peoples' home) in Eretz Yisroyel (Land of Israel).

From time to time he, or another indistinguishable from him, would appear, push his way in, lift off the box and shake it. If it was not heavy with coins he gave you a dirty look, berated you in no uncertain terms, hung the box back and stamped out.

Years later I would often walk along 47th Street, the diamond center in Manhattan. Many were the members of the tribe on that street, some with small black satchels, standing at the curb, making deals with big gestures of their hands and quick talk, walking in and out of buildings. Sometimes I would walk behind them and overhear their conversation. It was always commercial and sophisticated; often about the stock market.

An unforgettable member of the tribe was one for whom I delivered matzos—large crisp, square or round wafers ridged to break into neat strips, bubbly and dappled with the brown of their baking. They are made with unleavened flour. On Passover Jews may not eat leavened bread. Even matzos baked during the year may not be used. They must be "Kosher Shel Paysach"—that is, baked only after the bakery has been cleaned of every last crumb or shred of choomitz (leavened bread) presumably under the supervision of an ordained Rabbi.

This is a busy time for the Jewish housewife. The entire house must be cleaned spotless—the year-round dishes stored away or carefully segregated and a whole new set, used only for Paysach, brought out. In super Kosher houses the last crumbs of choomitz are cleaned out according to a set ritual. On the evening before the day of the first Saydir the baalabooss (master of the house) goes about the house in silence, with a lit candle, a dish and a feather. He brushes the last of the choomitz onto the dish. Before ten a.m. the next morning he takes the choomitz out and burns it.

In readiness for Paysach the grocery stores took large inventories of Paysachdicke matzos. Once when I was about eleven a kid who said he was from one of the newer tenements on Fox Street, came around and asked me and some other kids if we would like to earn fifty cents that night, helping to deliver matzos. We agreed. He said to wait on the corner. We did and soon a horse and wagon (ferd 'n voogin) drew up, driven by an old Jew with a long black coat, a white beard and a round hat.

We crowded into the wagon and were driven miles to some strange place in the Bronx. The wagon stopped at a dimly lit store with a "For Rent" sign in the window, empty, except for stacks of matzo box cartons piled from floor to ceiling. We helped load these on the wagon and jumped on ourselves. The horse trudged off, clip-clop, the old man flapping the reins to urge him on, stopping at store after store, delivering the cartons. Then we returned, loaded more, unloaded at stores and returned again. Trip after trip. The night wore on. Midnight had long passed. The cartons grew heavier and harder to lift. The piles in the storehouse diminished only slowly.

At last it was done. We were bone weary. We needed to go to the bathroom. We were bleary with lack of sleep. The old man told us to sit at the doorway of the now completely empty store. He had to go around the corner to get his money. He and the young recruiter got on the wagon and clopped off.

We waited and waited and waited. They never came back. God knows how and when we got home.

I remember that once one of the members of the tribe was in our kitchen rattling a Pushkeh he had taken from the side of the bathroom door, when he saw the clock on the kitchen shelf. Quickly he put down the Pushkeh and turned to me: "Ahvoo is ost?" (Where is east?) I hadn't the slightest idea, but I pointed. He faced in that direction, clasped his hands in front of his chest and, bobbing quickly up and down, raced through the evening prayer in a jumble of muttered noises. Then he put the Pushkeh back, cursed us and left.

One day I was playing stoopball in front of the house when one of the tribe came by, grabbed me by the wrist with an iron clasp, yanked me toward him and asked, "Vere is Vendivver Avenyeh?" I said I didn't know. He flung me from him, almost knocking me down, and said with contempt, "varridey titchin you in skool?"

Whether the Aybershter (the Lord above) ever punished the matzo goniff (crook) I don't know. But there was one whom the Aybershter had smitten mightily enough to make up for a great many sins of the tribe. This one was the father of a schoolmate. The boy was always neatly groomed, with blond hair, blue eyes and delicate pink skin. He was a gentle boy who avoided the street and bodily contact with other kids. But he boasted about his erector set, his super chemistry kit, his whole array of devices for spending time at home. I think now that he may have been a hemophiliac.

I visited his apartment several times. His father was one of the tribe, classically garbed and bearded. What he did on going to bed I do not know, but in the house and on the hottest days he wore the long black coat and round brimmed hat he wore outside. The old man owned the tenement they lived in. At home he was brusquely spoken and demanding. I would imagine his peremptory knock at the doors at rent collection time and his surly behavior counting bills and handing out receipts.

Blessed as he was in real estate, he was cursed otherwise. My friend was the youngest of twelve children. All the rest were girls. And none was married. Except for the "parlor" and kitchen I never saw the rest of the apartment. But girls crawled all over it. Wherever you looked they were there, doing homework, sewing, carrying laundry in and out of the bathroom, whirring a sewing machine somewhere in the dim recesses of the place, rattling dishes in the kitchen, sitting over tea or coffee and a book or a newspaper, never less than four or five moving about at the same time.

Somehow the presence of a strange male, even me at the threshold of pubescence, excited these girls. I was a pet. "Doesn't he have cute dimples!" "He's going to be a lady-killer!" "If you were a bird I would put salt on your tail and catch you!" etc.

On my first visit the father interrogated me: Had my parents yet made for me a shiddach (arranged for my marriage). "No." Did I go to Chayder? Actually I did go, on and off, when not stealing away to work after school or just play hooky. "Yes." The man smiled "A reechtiger shayner kadischle." (A right nice little prayer for the dead.) To many Jews there is no after-life except in the memory of those they leave behind. The memory of a son is precious. A pious man's desire for a son is, in part, his desire to have an assured kadisch— the prayer for the dead —said for him when the time comes. A father sometimes refers to a son as "My Kadisch.") What did my father do? "He's a butcher." The old man nodded approvingly. That connoted both affluence and froomkeit (the state of being religious).

In reality my father had neither of these attributes.

Some of the girls were intelligent and articulate. In a very short time they discovered that I was reading G. Stanley Hall's monumental work on adolescence. "Nathan dear, it's ad-oh-les-cence, not ah-dahl-iscince." They discovered that I had found the George Bernard Shaw shelf at the Library. Then they would preempt me, and my friend was left alone, sulking over his erector set.

Shortly after the beginning of training for my bar mitzvah (the ceremony of induction into Jewry of the thirteen year old boy) I dropped Chayder for good. It had never appealed to me in any case. The teaching was abominable and more time was spent on injecting us with Zionist fervor than teaching us to read and write Hebrew. I felt silly being made to walk around the classroom waving a small blue and white flag and singing the Jewish National Anthem: "Kaw-awl-oyd-bah-lay-vov, pinee-ee-ee ee-maw, lawshoov, vee eretz haw-aw-dee-ee maw!" I didn't then and I don't now know what the words mean. A national homeland? Fox Street was my national homeland. I found it unpleasant and frustrating to be given a passage from Torah to be learned by rote (in fact by sound alone) without understanding most of the words and when I asked questions be met brusquely with "Understand later. Learn now." The combination of Chayder and the tribe was more than enough to secularize me.

When my friend's father learned I was not to be bar-mitzvahed he pointed at me the next time he saw me in the house and screamed. "Aroiss fin mein

hoiss pahskootsve goy!" (Out of my house, disgusting gentile.)

At school my pink-faced friend avoided me. But
when any of the girls met me on the street she would
stop and chat.

THE BLIND MAN

South on Fox Street was a row of apartment houses built on lots that were empty when we moved there. In one of these lived a blind man. He could not have been over thirty. He was always neatly dressed, wore a jacket in even the hottest weather and although he had a strong face with red curly hair and a prominent chin, it was marred with a look of concern as he tapped his way down the block. Sometimes I helped him to cross streets—so he knew my voice and my touch.

One day he asked me if I would do him a favor. He wanted to move, and his wife insisted on a place with good light and a pleasant view. She worked during the day. Would I go with him to the West Bronx to look at some apartments whose addresses he had? I did. To my surprise the apartments he looked at were on the Grand Concourse, a wide boulevard that was the Park Avenue of the Bronx and so beautiful that Annie Besant, the English essayist, once called it one of the great boulevards of the Western World.

I described the layouts of the apartments, placed the windows for him and described the light and the view. He selected a large, handsome apartment with, among other things, a paneled study and built-in bar.

I never asked what he did for a living and always wondered about it. He was a well-spoken and apparently extremely intelligent man.

A year or so later, as I was riding in the subway, a beggar came through, tapping his way down the aisle and rattling coins in a tin cup. It was my blind man. At the end of the car he flipped the doors open and stepped through with greater assurance than I had ever seen in him going down a street.

OUR ITALIANS

The cutting of hair and the mending of shoes are two essential services in any neighborhood. In mine, as in many others in New York, they were given by men of Italian descent. By a joke of fate our barber was Mr. Martello, which I later learned means "hammer" and our shoe repair man—the "shoemaker"—was Mr. Capelli, which means "hairs."

Mr. Capelli

The shoemaker was a jovial, verbose little man with apple cheeks, dancing eyes and a long black mustache. He talked all the time, with broad gestures, even as he sat at his bench with his mouth full of shoe nails. Or he sang—preferably at his long machine (his building, on the other side of 156th, was electrified) where he could make his song fit the slapping and whirring of the belt as he burnished shoe uppers on the bristled wheels or smoothed down the edges of bottoms on the hard wheels. "C'e la luna mezz'o mare, Mamma mia, me maritari" or "La donna è mobile…"

I loved to be in his shop, to smell the fresh shoe leather and polish, to watch him maneuver a nail from his cheek to his lips, pick it out and, with one blow, wham it into the sole in a true line. Behind him was a wall painted with a crawling, poisonous blue, and marked with long cracks and bare plaster patches. But you could not see much of it. Most of it was covered with pictures of his heroes, torn from the front pages of magazines, or with lurid calendar art, some devotional and some very, very secular.

Those pictures left you in no doubt about who and what was near to his heart. Enrico Caruso, shown formally, with his big chin jutting forward, his mien dignified; or as a fat figure in velvet knickers, hands on sword and scabbard, a feather in his peaked cap; or in multi-colored clown garb, his eyes and mouth only faintly smeared so that his features were plain. The Pope, always formal, sometimes touching the cross on his chest. King Victor Immanuel with his pinched small face and piggy eyes, the high, round military hat and the decorations hanging like kitchen utensils on his small chest.

The calendar art was glossy and slick. Jesus opening his robe to show his red heart emitting golden rays; Jesus revealing a heart dripping perfectly formed drops of very red, non-staining blood; Mary crowned with a tiara of multi-colored jewels, standing tall on a small round world, her blue robe trimmed with gold thread, her hands in a gesture of blessing, her head bowed, her eyes down.

And the calendar ladies—their loose gossamer tunics falling to suggest the vast and creamy bosoms underneath; their heads tilted to feel the petals of red roses; their arms searching for the tops of marble pillars; their drapery hanging away from their smooth fat backs, down to the dimples that graced the creases of their buttocks.

I describe later an incident involving my older brother and the Pustleblatts who were anxious to have him as a husband for their daughter Yettie. Mr. Capelli, standing at his machine to finish off a pair of shoes he was repairing for me, spoke about it.

"Yoo bruddih, heesa-meck (then a gesture) wit' Yettie Poostallablahtta?" His gesture was big and plain. He held the shoe in one hand and pushed it forward while slapping at the upper arm with the other hand, "No? You bruddih he beddih watcha outa, oh Mrs. Poostallablahtta she poosha him ride on toppa her Yettie!"

Whenever Mr. Capelli spoke with a customer Mrs. Capelli would peek out from behind the curtain that separated the back from the front of the shop. If she saw that you noticed her, she pulled back. I don't know how many Capelli kids there were but sometimes you would see a few sitting quietly behind their father, skinny, with big, close-shaven heads, looking up with open mouths and wide, black eyes. You have seen these kinds of kids hundreds of times in appeals for money for depressed areas.

Mr. Martello

The barber was a quiet, immaculately groomed man, short, with a manner of elegant efficiency in the handling of his scissors. He managed, however, to dig his comb into your hair so hard that you winced, sure that he had ripped off a piece of scalp. "I hurta you? Sorry. Nexta time not so harda." His promise was worthless. He would keep attacking.

When he opened his shop in the morning Mr. Martello came out with a crank to wind up his barber pole. It would turn for hours, the red and white stripes spiraling endlessly upward. While he was cutting your hair the biggest part of his attention was at the window, watching, waving his scissors at passers-by. If he noticed that his pole had stopped turning he abandoned you abruptly and went to the back to get his crank.

He began by choking you with the covering sheet. His clippers pulled more hair from the back of your neck than they cut. When he was finished pulling and cutting he sprinkled your shorn hair with smelly green water and dug his fingers into your scalp to spread the stuff. Then he combed and brushed, forever it seemed, fighting down the last springy hair. He would stand back, head cocked, to study his handiwork. He went through the formality of holding a hand mirror to the back of your head as though you could ask for an alteration. If you had I am sure he would have looked at you with offended horror. At last he would unpin the sheet, flap out the cuttings and release you. You rose, your neck bare and chafed, your back itchy, feeling like somebody else. As you turned to leave the shop his eyes took on a glassy stare and he walked to the window to look out, torpid, his hands behind his back.

I assumed that Mr. Martello was not married. Twice a week at about closing time a short, ample lady with a large floppy velvet hat would visit with Mr. Martello and, after he locked the door and put out the lights, would disappear with him to the back of the shop. Who was she? I had to wait my turn once while a grown-up was in the chair. "Say Luigi, was that your wife I saw coming in here last night?" "My *wife*? Dunn bee coorehzy. That prostituta! She good owny for a quick premere."

Maybe he *was* married.

I don't know whether it was this ill-concealed activity of Mr. Martello or plain naughtiness that provoked the kids, sometimes, to stand at his door and shout: "Barber, barber, shave my larber." (referring to hairy genitals). Mr.

Martello was wise. He let them yell themselves weary. The chant would soon die down and they would go off, not to appear again for a long time.

MR. BRILL'S PEN

For a long time after we moved to Fox Street Mr. Brill was the nearest druggist. His shop was a typical one of the time. Apart from a small candy rack featuring mostly cough drops the store was dominated by the necessaries of the pharmacist. Behind the counter were shelves with round heavy china jars trimmed with gold and carrying the perplexing abbreviations we used to wonder at: "Cl Bmnx," "Hp Fpl," "Nu Vom," "Pot As," etc.

In the glass-covered shelves at the front of the counter were the sick room accessories; ear syringes, enema bags, bedpans, thermometers, etc. You felt that if you needed anything but toothpaste from that store you were really sick.

Hanging on chains in Mr. Brill's windows were the large, long, pointed-bottom glass jars filled with red, green and blue liquid. Those jars were to the druggist what the red and white-spiraled pole was to the barber and the three gold balls to the pawnbroker.

My mother liked Mr. Brill because he was so professional looking and so absolutely certain about the proper remedy for anything. For me it was mostly magnesia (a colorless bubbly draught of nauseating taste) or castor oil, that disgusting cathartic whose taste nothing could hide, certainly not the few drops of orange juice squeezed on the spoon.

Mr. Brill was short and always wore neat, grey suits and white shirts. His pointed shoes were of shiny patent leather. When he attended you he stood behind the counter, his hands resting on it, his head down, so that you could count the sparse hairs brushed sideways over his shiny pate, and he looked at you over his glasses. He rarely gave a verbal acknowledgment of your request. If you asked him for a remedy for some ailment he would turn, pull a box or a bottle out of a drawer behind him, pass it to you and say, "Three times a day before meals. Thirty cents."

My married sister made an uncle of me when I was about six. Since my mother frequently left me alone I spent much time with my sister, who lived about a block away. And since she lived on the top floor, I was a welcome pair of legs. I was sent often to the drugstore. Once I was sent for "limewater." I watched, wondering, as Mr. Brill put some clear liquid into a beaker and, with a pipette bubbled his breath into it. As he did, the liquid became cloudy. He poured it into a bottle, labeled it and handed it over.

To me the most intriguing thing about Mr. Brill was his fountain pen. He carried it in the outside breast pocket of his jacket. It was a Waterman's—slender, black, with open-work silver applique on the barrel and cap. The gold tip was always shiny. Mr. Brill handled his pen like a master. He would whip it out of his pocket, expose the point, place the cap at the end and write in a quick and elegantly slanting hand. The cap was then removed, replaced, fastened with a twist and the pen reclipped in the pocket with a single graceful motion. The entire act had the beauty of simplicity and efficiency. No panache, no frills. I got, from watching him use his pen, the same thrill that Francescotti gave me years later when I saw and heard him play the first movement of Beethoven's Spring Sonata—smooth, fluent, lovely.

One of the shameful moments of my life occurred in Brill's drug store. While he was in the back packing some Seidlitz powders I was getting for my father I filched a box of Smith Brothers licorice cough drops. My heart was in my mouth. I couldn't get out of the store fast enough. Although licorice was my favorite flavor I got no enjoyment from the cough drops. I brooded. The next day I made a special trip to Brill's and said, with my head hanging. "I took a box of cough drops and forgot to pay." I pushed a nickel across the counter. Mr. Brill looking at me over his glasses pushed the nickel back. "I know. Don't do it again," he said gently.

THE KOSHER BUTCHER

My father was a kosher butcher. As far as I know he never worked as a butcher for anyone else or hired a butcher to work for him. He would run a one-man butcher shop. His stores were rarely successful. In good part this was because of the way he treated women: insolently.

My father once said that his father, grandfather and great grandfathers had been kosher butchers for as many generations back as anyone can remember and for many generations in the same stall in a market in or near Czernowitz, Bukovina.

My father was extraordinarily skilled. He was interested in anatomy, knew the shape and function of every muscle and organ in a beef or chicken, and if he didn't know (as for example two small fatty nodules on either side of a chicken's coccyx), didn't rest until he found out. He told me about these nodules, but I don't remember. He could traber (devein a hindquarter) neatly without spilling a drop of blood or wasting meat. He claimed (and I believe it) that he could do it with his eyes closed.

I would watch him, absorbed, as he threw a quarter of beef on the block and dismembered it, his sharp knife, with precise ripping noises, following down the clean, shiny linings of the muscles or tracing the outlines of bone, his cleaver making exactly placed single whacks, his saw neatly severing the bone at the right place.

He was an expert buyer. Sometimes when I was very young he would wake me at five in the morning and take me down to the slaughterhouse—then on the East Side in Midtown Manhattan. It was a large, barn-like structure. The steers were penned in layers of corrals on one side. Big black men would enter a pen, lash the fore and hind feet of the animal and lift it head down onto a giant hook swinging from a rail in the ceiling. They would give it a push and the animal, flailing about, would ride down to the center of the room. There, on a raised cement platform, stood the shoychitt (slaughterer) a large man with massive arms, wearing a rubber apron, an enormous knife in his hand. Near him was a gushing spout and about the platform was a gutter. The slaughterer would catch the animal by the mouth as it neared him, arch its neck and make a single large cut—almost to the spine. A sudden gush of blood into the gutter, a violent twitching of the animal's body, and it was pushed off on the rail to be beheaded, skinned and disemboweled.

(The kosher slaughter of chickens was, in a way, much crueler. The shoychitt was an ordained Rabbi and dressed like one. He would stand over a large empty drum with an open barber's razor in his hand. His assistant would reach into the coop, grab a chicken and hand it to the shoychitt with its wings pressed to its body. The shoychitt would tuck the chicken under his arm, bend the head back, ruffle the feathers under the neck and make a quick pass, severing the windpipe. Then he would press upward on the windpipe so that its end projected out of the neck. All this happened very fast and, in the excitement, the chicken probably forgot to breathe. When it was dumped into the barrel it crouched, looked around resentfully until it realized it couldn't breathe. Then it would go through an agony of strangulation until, a long time later, it died.)

Back to the steers: After this preliminary dressing (odd way to refer to the undressing of the steer) it would be rolled into a cold house and hung, stiff, last in a line of carcasses.

It was here that the buying was done. My father would pass along the rows of carcasses, avoiding the salesmen who were taking orders from other buyers and, when he found the carcass he wanted, would slide a large switch blade from his pocket and slice slabs of fat from the back, where it would not be noticed, and tossed them into a corner. He would order delivery from that carcass.

My father treated customers abominably. His meat was fresh. But he believed in high prices. He would say of a nearby competitor, "Rabinovitz fumfkit schoin nuch a mool mit de prizen!" (Rabinowitz is horsing around again with his prices!) to express anger at his competition.

I once actually witnessed, live, in my father's shop a dialogue which I heard in later life as a joke:

Lady to butcher: "You hev lemb chops?"

Butcher: "Yeah."

Lady: "How mahch?"

Butcher: "Eighty five cents ah pond."

Lady: "Rabinowitz is chonging seventy nine."

Butcher: "So why don't you buy by Rabinowitz?"

Lady: "He's ahlt of lemb chops right nah."

Butcher: "Lady! Ven I'm ahlt of lemb chops my prize is sixty-nine cents!"

The perennial tug of war between butcher and customer in a kosher shop was over the amount of fat the butcher failed to trim off before weighing the meat. My father had his own standards and could not be moved. Scenes like this were common:

"Mr. Lowbull nemmt aroop de fets." (Take off the fat.)

"Zorgt ach nit. Ich nem aroop." (Don't worry. I take off.) He would lay the meat on the scale, weigh it, and then take it down and trim off a smidgeon more fat.

"Mr. Lowbull, vaegst es noch a mool." (Weigh it again!)

Then my father would look her straight in the eye, lift the meat from the counter and drop it neatly into the waste can. That was the politest thing he would do. At times he would say: "Missis, kahkt aich oop!" (Madam, beshit yourself!) or "Kisht meer in toochis!" (Kiss my ass!) and sit down calmly to read his newspaper.

Once a woman came in late in the afternoon and asked for six lamb chops. Instead of serving her, my father put his hands against the top of the showcase and said, with some heat, "Missis, eyer mann teet oop a schvathen took arbit. Fer sitzt a guntsin took mit eyer yentiss. Er kimmt ahame in vill a gitten teller zoop in a git schtick flaysh, nit a tsikrochenne klayper lemb chop. Nit beir meer vett eer kriggen lemb chops hulb nooch feer!" (Mrs. your man does a hard day's work. You sit all day with your gossipy friends. When he comes home he wants a good plate of soup and a good hunk of meat. Not a puckered little lamb chop. Not from me will you get lamb chops at four-thirty.)

I suspected he had no lamb chops in the shop.

Long after we moved from Washington Avenue where

82

I was born, my father took a butcher stall in a market on that street. By then many blacks had moved into the area. My father was ruthlessly dishonest with them. He bought the lowest grades of meat for sale. He overweighed. One trick was to bag the purchase, put the bag on the scale with the open flap facing you and pull down on the flap with a finger. He made dishonest charges. The trick was to write down the cost of items on the bag, reach an over-stated total with lightning movements of the pencil and the lips, tear the bag as you pushed the meat in—and then, of course, give the customer a fresh bag.

My father, however, made up for much with his smoked meats. He had Mr. Midzhick the tinsmith make a small smoke house for him. This he set on one of his blocks and he would begin, early in the morning, to smoke lean pastrami and other meats. He used to go to Bronx Park on Saturday, when kosher butchers were closed, and gather baskets full of aromatic woods which he used in the smokehouse. He used the freshest, best cuts for smoking. He spiced them expertly. By noon the Washington Avenue market was filled with the delicious smells of his smokehouse and his steady customers, the keepers of other stalls, came to him slavering to buy slices for their lunch sandwiches. He was proud of his smoked meats, gave generous weights, charged reasonably, and glowed at the compliments of his customers.

Among the meats he smoked were lamb shanks. He rubbed these liberally with spices and smoked them un-til the meat was stiff along the bone. These he would bring home at night and simmer overnight and all the next day in a large kettle of water and kidney beans. By the next evening the meat was tender and away from the bones and the beans mushy and fragrant with the smoked spices. He would cook up a mess of cornmeal mush (mamaliga) and dump it into the hollow he had made in a large slab of oak trunk. So expert was he that the meal came clean out of the pot, leaving it spotless. On top of the mamaliga went the meat and beans and you ate it by spooning out combinations of mamaliga with "darrflayshn fanrsawlyiss." He had learned the recipe from the shepherds in the Carpathian Mountains.

My Uncle Noosin, on my father's side, and his children were and generations later have remained butchers. A prominent shop in Midtown Manhattan is their outlet. They are very fancy and expensive, catering to the rich and writing books about meat. I wonder if any one of them can traber.

Having told you this much about the kosher butcher I feel I ought to tell you more. The koshering of meat is done by rubbing the large chunk (from which the meat will be cut for sale) with coarse salt and washing the salt off with running water. The meat must be wet fresh. It is never aged. Unless you chop or boil kosher meat it is likely to be as tough as it is wholesome.

The installation of butcher fixtures was sometimes done by the "fat man"—the rendering company that periodically emptied the metal pails into which scraps of fat, bone, or, if a calf's head had been trimmed, skin were thrown. The butcher got a meager allowance for this waste. The rest of the "muggidge" on his fixtures he paid periodically in cash.

Butcher stores had walk-in cold storage rooms—the "eiz" box. From time to time a butcher would try to place his grinder in the eiz box and, when preparing chopped meat for a customer, would cut the slab on the block, carry it into the box and then bring out the ground beef. This never lasted long. The customers were cagey and refused to take the risk that the butcher would substitute scraps for the fresh cut. And so, reluctantly, the grinder would be placed where it could be seen. My father made a big play of his honesty with the grinder. He left it in plain view. Before putting in the customer's meat he would run a piece of fat through the grinder, push out the fragments of the last grind, wipe them away and toss in the fresh cut. He always stood to one side when he did this, so the customer could watch.

Butchers used two-faced hanging scales with white porcelainized trays. The scales always had a small red seal at the center showing that they had been inspected. Nevertheless many scales were dishonest. Under the housing of the balances or springs was a small metal bulb which could be unscrewed. This bulb had tiny metal pellets, used to true up the zero point of the scale. By removing the bulb and changing the pellets you could under weigh by a substantial amount. Inspections were infrequent; not all inspectors were honest, and fines were moderate. It paid to tamper.

My father was an uncanny judge of weights. He could, by hefting a piece of meat, tell you within an ounce how much it weighed. Sometimes he made a game of this. He would cut a slice, lay it on a sheet of paper on his hand and say, "Van pahnd tree qvudders, last ah nahntz" or "ah funt drei drei fertel leicht ah noontz." Then he would throw it on the counter to wrap it. If he got a quizzical look from the customer, he would ask, "You dun believe?" or "Eer glaybt nit?" and throw it on the scale. He had called the weight accurately according to the scale since he had already adjusted the weight he gave for the error of the scale.

According to my father my Uncle Noosin was an expert with weights. He would hold a lead sinker concealed in his hand and slip it into a chicken carcass before weighing. He would drop the sinker back into his hand before bagging the chicken.

SOME FAMILIES

The Midzhiks

Our second floor apartment had no street front. The kitchen window looked out at the yard, the hollow of a "U" made by 744 Fox and the back of the first tenement around the corner.

Directly across from us were the rear windows of the Midzhiks who lived in the adjoining tenement. The Midzhiks had three children—all boys and none older than nine. All the Midzhiks were darkly complected. Mrs. Midzhik was an overweight woman with straight black hair, a Mongolian face and slanted eyes. She was dumpy, always wore dirty housedresses and sneakers over socks rolled down to her ankles. She was what my father would call a "zhlupp." Mr. Midzhick was a tin-smith. He was slender and neat and gently spoken. He made for my father the sheet-metal smokehouse, which my father praised. My father was an excellent craftsman himself and his praise was something to earn.

Mr. Midzhik was a baalmaloochih (a master of his craft) and an ahnshtendigger mann (a respectable man).

The little Midzhiks were jumping fleas. They were all skinny and dark, their hair was close shaven and from our kitchen we could see them bounce about in silhouette— between their back and front windows. So often did Mrs. Midzhik scream and grab at one just as he was spilling off the windowsill that we no longer looked to see what was happening.

87

The most remarkable thing about the family was its smell. Each and every one of the Midzhik kids was a bed-wetter. I was in their apartment once. The smell was so powerful that I became nauseated and left quickly. Mrs. Midzhik must never have bathed. When she passed in the street a strong trail of body and urine smells followed in her wake. My father often shook his head and muttered, of Mr. Midzhik, "Veezoi kenn er's oseladen?" (How can he stand it?)

From time to time Mrs. Midzhik performed an act that, in any civilized country, would be an enjoinable nuisance. She draped the boys' mattresses over her airshaft windowsills. Within a short time the stink pervaded the narrow, dead air space. Nobody complained. But even on the hottest day you could hear windows being slammed shut all around the yard.

The Pustleblatts

They lived on Fox Street, but on the "other" side of 156th. They were thus semi-foreigners. Since I once heard Mr. Brill, the druggist, refer to a pus boil as a "pustleblatt" I knew what their name meant. Thus they revolted me without any need for further provocation. But they were revolting enough in their own right. Mr. Pustleblatt was a furrier—a fact that gave him status in that little community and that hinted at affluence. He was a short, loud-mouthed man who preempted the fruit-box conversations on hot nights with talk of his rich "kahstimmers" and his "intvesmins." Mrs. Pustleblatt was a kinky haired woman with a loud voice and large gold teeth. She was a reputation mangler and a paranoid who saw insults in the flick of other people's eyes.

The Pustleblatts had a daughter—Yettie—and an ambition: to have Yettie marry a doctor. My brother Larry, fresh out of high school, was known to want to be a doctor. His blond hair, blue eyes, gentle manner and "proper" English led everyone to believe that he would make it (as indeed he did). And so the Pustleblatts latched on to my brother, flattered him, courted him, bowed to him, paraded their daughter before him and, more pertinently, made a business proposition to my mother. For a prompt engagement to Yettie they would pay his way through school until he was ready to practice, when they would fit him out with an office.

Yettie was a lumpy girl with bulging eyes and kinky hair like her mother's. She was the only girl who, in all my memory, I ever saw in a kicking, scratching and hair-pulling contest.

One of my mother's ambitions was to be a shatchinih (a marriage broker). She was as eager to start with my brother as a neophyte mutual fund salesman is to start with one of his relatives. My father put his foot down. Yettie was a "schloompigih, tziluzzinih moyt" (awkward, incompetent, slatternly girl). Mrs. Pustleblatt was a "marchzittzern" (a market sitting, soliciting slattern) and Mr. Pustleblatt was an "oongeshtupter nahr" (a bloated fool). Besides which the boy "Vet sich allane gefinnen a kahlih." (He'll find a bride by himself).

Larry never married Yettie.

The Krumwegs

The Krumwegs occupied one of the five flats on the second floor. Since we occupied another and Abie and I were of the same age it was natural that I should spend a lot of time in his flat. There were four Krumweg boys and two girls. Of the boys I remember most clearly Abie and Muttie, who was about three years younger. The very youngest boy was born while Abie and I played together. I had nothing to do with him. Abie was a serious, practical boy, not much given to games. Muttie was a street urchin, strong and strong-willed, with black curly locks and dancing eyes. He was a pest and a devil and the darling of the family. In the middle of anything he would rush up to anybody, say "Futtue" and scamper off. His brother Abie would say, "Aint he cute?" and if he could grab Muttie would offer his arm to you saying, "Feel him, he's salad as a rock!"

The oldest Krumweg boy was out of public school—as likely expelled as graduated. He was the "bad one," had been arrested several times (I never knew for what) and was said to be destined to be a "gengster." He worked on the truck of a wholesale clothes dry cleaner, making pick-ups from small tailor shops, including his own father's shop, which happened to be in the building in which we lived. Every time he called at his father's shop there was yelling. "Vee bistih gevayn letzte nacht? Dry azayger is a tsite ahametzikimmin?" (Where were you last night? Three o'clock is a time to come home?)

"Ah, mind your fucken business. I bring home my paydih (wages) don't I?" Then a roar: "Tzin a footer zugt min nitt 'fucken' du bestidd du!" (To a father you don't say "fucken" you bastard you!)

Mrs. Krumweg was a plain, pleasant and peasant-like woman, very easy on herself and others. Little things I remember. I could come and go without knocking. She was willing to listen to me read from my first reader: "Dickey Dare went to school. On the way he met the cow. Moo said the cow." She fed us goodies. One was dry powdered cocoa mixed with sugar which she spooned into our mouths as we sat around her kitchen table. All kitchen tables were white with porcelainized metal tops, plain square legs and two drawers for knives, forks, etc .

Mr. Krumweg, the tailor, was a short, thin man with close cropped greying hair, prominent cheekbones, small widely-spaced teeth and a seamed face. His most prominent features were his ears. They were large, very large, and thin and round and they stuck out at right angles from his head. He was often at his sewing machine, running it at whirring speed or sitting sideways at it, hand stitching with quick precise movements. He threaded needles and bit off thread faster than anyone else I ever saw. Or he would be at his pressing machine, pushing down on the pedal and pulling down on the bar on the top flap of the machine, sending bursts of steam through the cloth lining of the pressing boards. That steam made the air damp, oppressive in the summer and lovely in the winter, and had a slightly sharp, pleasant smell.

In the winter, when it was cold outside, Krumweg's store window was clouded with steam so that you could see only the halo of the bulbs that hung exposed over his presser and his sewing machine. I would stand at that window for a long time trying to look in, or watching drops of water form in the steam coating on the window and make their erratic, darting way down to the bottom.

The most interesting and forceful Krumweg was Rosie, the oldest girl. She must have been about three years older than Abie and I. I remember her dressing "fancy" to go to her public school graduation while we were still in the fifth grade.

Rosie was positive and adventurous. When I was about ten and she thirteen she organized a "Show." She had the boys build a round amphitheater with lumber lying about the construction sites on the block. She was general contractor, organizer and expediter. When we had the theatre built she was producer, ringmaster and star. She introduced the acts. She recited. She sang, positively, clearly and out of tune:

> *It was at the bullfight I met her.*
> *It was at the daring display.*
> *I went down to get some peanuts and programs*
> *When the dirty bum stole her away.*
> *He shall die; he shall die; he shall die*
> *Diddley-ey-die-dee-die.*
> *I'll plant an onion on his Spanish bunion*
> *When the dirty bum lies in his grave.*

One of the hit acts was "Prince—the Singing Dog." The Krumwegs had a sharp-nosed, twitchy little dog called Prince. This wretched animal would sit at your feet, look up and emit loud and painful whines when you played a harmonica in the upper register. If you shooed him away and kept on playing he would come back and whine again.

I have come to think that Rosie's ideas had literary sources. Isn't there an almost exactly similar sequence in Booth Tarkington, down to the alternate prices she charged for admission—two cents or ten pins?

Rosie married early. A "wise guy" character, who

came with all the sophistication of the Broadway gutter. He operated a candy and cigarette stand in a crumby hotel in the theatre district. He lived with the Krumwegs. How did they manage to squeeze all those people into the place? With his flat, sharp nose, jutting jaw and cold eyes he would humble us younger ones with his fast talk and up-to-date lingo. Rosie worked with him at the candy stand and once she recruited us to work for them. The work consisted of going along Broadway handing out circulars advertising, of all things, a production at the Metropolitan Opera House of Richard Strauss' *Salome*— "See the Daring Dance of the Seven Veils."

The Hills

The Hills occupied the "middle" apartment on our floor—all front windows. Mr. Hill was a tall, thin man with a large and very shiny bald head. He would stand out even if silent—for he had a thin, hooked nose that jutted prominently out of his face and a jaw that receded so markedly as to come close to meeting his neck on the direct slant. Also, he was always "formally" dressed. He wore high celluloid collars, false cuffs with large cufflinks and striped shirts. He smoked cigars and (I suppose because of his receding lower jaw) rarely had his cigar in his mouth except to puff at it. Otherwise he held it delicately in his hand (a large gold ring on one finger) with his pinkie crooked. He tenderly cultivated long ashes.

He had only to speak to mark himself out from all the others. His speech was Cockney to a T, with "r"s that sounded more like "w"s, because his lips rarely closed over a consonant. His speech was all the more remarkable because it was peppered with Yiddish words spoken with his strange accent.

It was obvious when Mr. Hill came home from work with his dapper clothes and clean hands that he was no laborer. In fact Mr. Hill was an artist. He hand-decorated expensive china. He was born and had studied art in England and had very positive ideas about art education. When he found out that I was drawing with charcoal he was shocked. "The 3B pencil—that's your tool, boy! Force yourself to be exact—make a clean line. Wotten show for twaining, this charcoal fuzz!"

Mrs. Hill was a vapid, cleanly dressed woman with frizzly light hair and watery blue eyes. She sat out with the others on warm nights, fanning herself languidly with a woven bamboo fan. Her conversation was limited to short and somewhat snide remarks about the prevalent lack of manners in the United States generally and on Fox Street particularly.

The Hills had a daughter, Emily, about my age. I rarely played with Emily and never, except once, went into the Hills' apartment. That once was at Mr. Hill's invitation—to show me a portrait he was doing of Emily. There it was, a long narrow canvas on an easel near a window: Emily, in a ruffled white dress, short sleeves with pink ribbons, a short bob, white socks and black patent leather shoes, staring at me resentfully. It wasn't great art. But it was Emily.

It was obviously not finished. And from the looks of it, compared to Emily at the time I saw the portrait, it had been started a considerable time before. Mr. Hill saw me scan the painting—and read my thoughts. He waved at it, cigar in hand, and said—"Not finished." Then he looked down and said, "So little time." I didn't know what he meant until months later when he was taken to a hospital, not to return.

The Szabars

The Szabars lived around the corner on 156th Street. Their stoop was a favored gathering place of adolescents. The sidewalk in front of my stoop on Fox Street was always crowded with husbands and wives sitting on fruit boxes or on folding wooden chairs, yacking. There were two attractions to the 156th Street stoop. One was the streetlight directly in front of it. We tended to gather like moths around the street light posts. The other was Frankie Klein (who is described later in this book), an aesthete who spoke like a Harvardian.

I fix the years of gatherings on that stoop by the fact that in one of those years, 1927, Lindbergh flew the Atlantic. Cynics and sophisticates though we thought we were, we caught the fever of excitement over his feat and even called him "Lindy."

One of those who gathered on that stoop was Magda Szabar. She had a brother who was near her age—Zoltan. Her father, Bela, was a short, dumpy man with a fat nose and thick lips, a large bristling mustache, plentiful black hair and bulging, poached eyes. Her mother was short and dainty, with an oval face, olive complexion, dancing dark eyes and a rather long but elegant nose who wore her enormously long black hair in a thick braid wound around her head.

Magda had a flat chest, short, mousy hair, a hooked

nose and two front teeth that projected out so straight that she could not, except with effort, close her lips over them. But she was bright and witty, and had some charm—mainly because of her slight and pleasant foreign accent and her continental way of seeing and commenting on things. She had travelled and made no pride of it, so she was interesting and more than tolerable company. We all felt that though she would have loved to be necked, we could not go that far to oblige her. It was, I think, her teeth. You felt that they would pierce you in a kiss.

Magda must have told her parents what a nice, gentlemanly and very artistic boy I was. And so her mother, returning from shopping, would pause on the stoop and say "hello" to me. One day she noticed a book lying next to me as I sat on the stoop wall. It was Nietzsche's *Thus Spake Zarathustra*. Mrs. Szabar looked at me with wonder and admiration. "You are reeding thees book?" When she found out that I was, indeed, she became my fast friend.

Before I go any farther I must tell you more about the father, Bela. Sometimes he would stand on the stoop listening to us kids. Mostly he was silent. But from time to time he would utter a quick, positive sentence in a thick Hungarian accent. It was always a pronouncement, and always the same—a piece of Communist dogma. For example, on Lindbergh: "Zis is ah cop-eht-ah-list preparahtzion for ze imperialistische vohr ahgenst de vurrkers of de vurrld!" At election time, "Foolish pipples is teenking dot is any deefferengs bitveen vun pahrrty and anudderr. All zie same cop-eht-ah-list leckeys."

Some time later I was told by Mrs. Szabar that Bela, a brilliant student, had been expelled from school because of his seditious views and that, in fact, they had left Hungary to escape prosecution. She hinted more than once that his brilliance and profundity were far beyond her; that his learning was stupendous. I never saw or heard any evidence of this. He worked as an editorial writer for a radical paper printed in Hungarian. I surmised that these editorials were, like his conversation, nothing but strings of party slogans, trite to me even then (who had grown up in this neighborhood that rocked with the boil of union politics and rang with the shouts and mutual recriminations of the linkes (leftists) and rechtes (rightists). I tried often to lead Mr. Szabar into conversation about non-political ideas. It was hopeless. Before he finished a sentence he was citing Marx or Engels or Lenin in a singsong chant that was like the babbling of a Rabbi over the scroll of the Torah. I was repelled by Bela Szabar's mind and speech and I think, in part, that he was one of the reasons why doctrinaire radicalism never appealed to me.

Mr. Szabar did not get along with his son. Zoltan had no interest in politics, in books, in anything but automobiles. He wanted to quit school and become a mechanic. Each parent had a separate reason for being shocked: Bela because his son wanted to be an *actual* worker (ze clahss vitch, soonehr or latehrr vill rih-ool ze vurrld); Mrs. Szabar because Zoltan, instead of showing any aesthetic bent, was a surly peasant.

Both parents, I believe, shared this reason: I had been given to understand that each had come from a "berühmte" (distinguished) family and, without ever saying it, they made it clear that it was shocking that the skin of a body of these bloods should be soiled with grease.

Mrs. Szabar merely grieved. Mr. Szabar taunted, goaded, cursed his son and whipped up violent arguments with him. Magda would simply throw up her hands, "Oh… those two..."

Mrs. Szabar was the most fascinating of the family. She had trouble speaking English. I knew no Hungarian whatsoever. And so she spoke to me in a mixture of German and English which gave me very little trouble. Her voice was musical and easy to listen to. She had two main interests, and these were the main threads in her conversations with me; these interests were art and joy—primarily the joy of sex.

Before I go any further please understand that this lady was a gentlewoman and exceedingly proper. I suspect that she would have liked to see me engaged to her daughter. Probably to her mind there would be nothing strange in such an arrangement between a 15-year-old boy and a 14-year-old girl.

This suspicion was engendered in part by the continental character of the Szabars and of the milieu of their apartment. Their furniture was heavy, dark, shiny and ornately decorated. Their dining room table was covered with a richly woven cloth of paisley design with the colors of old wine, and elegant little glints of gold thread around the curved shapes of the design. The large bureau had a mirrored back against which were arranged plates with scalloped, gold-trimmed edges and with ornately painted scenes from elegant 18th century life. Mrs. Szabar served hot chocolate in octagonal shaped pink and blue cups with gold trimmings. Her tableware was of heavy silver with large and intricately designed handles.

It was very fine, very exotic and different. But I feared that it was just the kind of atmosphere in which a troth between an eager Magda and a softened me could be plighted and blessed. After a while I felt choked in that apartment.

While my visits lasted my conversations with Mrs. Szabar were absorbing. We talked while Magda sat between us, chin on hand, drumming her fingers on the table. Often during our conversations we could hear arguments in the kitchen, emerging in a low roar, between Zoltan and his father. Sometimes they would erupt into shouts and table banging. Then Mrs. Szabar would wince, close her eyes and pause until the shouting and banging subsided.

Mrs. Szabar's interests in art and sex were two ships on the strong current of her belief in joy and her willingness to enjoy. Over and over she would say, "Ich bin so für Art!" or "Wass ein shame dass du nicht ein Frau war! Then you vood know dass die höchste Freude (highest joy)—und est ist wirklich ein sexualische Freude—ist ein Kind zugebären. I mean to give the birth to the baby; die ecstase to feel the coming out by the child of the body!" Or, "Hast du mal gelesen (read) Otto Weininger's *Geschlecht und Charackter* (Gender and Character)? Ein buch for you." I in turn recommended to her Havelock Ellis' *Man and Woman*.

She showed me her work: some pretty, characterless watercolors of flowers and some pieces of an unusual type. It looked like dull tapestry. It was made with crayons heavily applied to burlap and heated with a pressing iron to melt the colored waxes. What could be done with this technique I can't say. Her work was stiff and dull.

The Szabars just passed out of my life. Whether they moved from the neighborhood or I did, or when, I cannot say.

But there is an epilogue. Some time after I lost touch with them I heard that Zoltan had stabbed his father in the neck with an ice pick.

The Kleins

One of the pivots in my life was Frankie Klein, who lived around the corner on 156th Street. His father was Abe Klein; his mother was Rose; his sister was Ciel, Lucille or Celia, I never knew which, and his brother was Morris. Abe was a spare man with deep-set eyes, a prominent chin, a small bulb for a nose, a close-cropped greying mustache and neatly combed greying dark hair. I visited at the house often, but rarely did I fail to find him at the kitchen or the dining room table, sewing ties. Abe was the head tailor in the robe-making department of an extremely exclusive and expensive firm of haberdashers. He would bring home ends of the silks used for robes and sew ties with them. As far as I know he never sold any. He just kept himself busy. The silks were of gorgeous weaves and textures. But they were much too flamboyantly printed for my taste, so, although I had the world's costliest silk ties pressed on me, I very rarely wore one.

Abe was a gracious and patient man. I never saw him angry or heard him raise his voice. Rose was a short and very heavy woman with exceedingly fair skin and watery grey eyes. Her nose was straight and prominent, her chin full and her mouse-colored hair carried in a short bob—so that the crease where her neck met her back stared at me while she attended the stove or the sink and spoke in her thin, complaining voice.

Rose was not a talkative woman. She opened up only once. At the kitchen table drinking tea, while Abe sat sewing ties, she reminisced about her days as a green-horn (a fresh immigrant). At first she and Abe lived with a couple they had known in their village in Russia. As soon as Abe got a job, in a garment "place," they rented a flat on the top floor of an East Side tenement. Abe described the garment place: a crowded walk-down-store run by a man and wife who treated workers as tiniff (garbage, dregs) and didn't allow you time "zich tzu vischen dem hinten" (to wipe your behind).

While Abe was out working Rose spent almost all her time in the flat. The crowds and the noises of the street frightened her. A few days after they moved in she heard a voice calling loudly in the halls and on the stairs, "Koylen! Koylen!" That is a Yiddish word meaning "slaughter." It means also "coals." It was, in fact, the man with the sack of coals who filled your bucket for cooking at the black stove. But fresh in Rose's memories were the cries made during pogroms by someone running through the village shouting, "Loyft! Loyft! Mih koylit Yeedin!" (Run! Run! They're slaughtering Jews!) To her the word could have only one meaning. And so, she told us, she flattened herself under the bed and lay there, trembling, hour after hour, until Abe came home.

When she told this story her eyes danced and she

slapped her hands on her thighs. You could feel how intensely grateful she was to be able to sit in her kitchen in the Bronx, secure, free of the fear of pogroms.

Ciel was the "bright" one of the family. She was short, had a large but straight and turned-up nose and a very prominent chin. She was intelligent, enthusiastic and quick in speech. She wore her hair in a very mannish bob, wore very short skirts and was to a "T" the very modern Millie. She was ample (one could see her destiny in her mother's frame) but her ankles were trim, she stood straight and held her head high and one could see that someone (not I) could find her desirable.

Ciel worked as a stenographer. One of her jobs was at Krasman's Foods. She worked for young Mr. Krasman. While she would make fun of his fancy shirts and pointed shoes, it was obvious that she held him as "boss" with all this might (but I am sure did not) imply.

While I was still a frequent visitor at the Klein's, Ciel married a good-looking, good-natured and bright young man whose first and second names were identical with those of a then prominent songwriter. As fate would have it, Ciel's husband's ambition was to be a songwriter and at the time of their marriage he was preparing a batch of lyrics to show around. Since he could not yet see his ship in harbor, he and Ciel lived temporarily with the Kleins. This interim arrangement lasted as long as I knew them.

Law as a profession was then as distant from my mind as was chicken sexing. But Ciel's husband, for some reason, asked me whether his established namesake would have the right to prevent the newcomer from using his own name on published songs. I did not know the answer then, and after a career as a lawyer and to some extent a legal scholar, I still do not know the answer.

Morris Klein was the older brother. He was blond, blue-eyed and had a short, thin nose with widely flaring nostrils. He was nervous— always twitching and squirming and twisting his neck. He rarely joined us at conversations and, when he did, his jerky manner and drawled, whining speech threw a pall over us. He was the dark side of the family. The intimations were that he was a "genius" who could have gone far. But he suffered from frequent and agonizing headaches and would retire to a dark room and lie flat on his back with a cold cloth over his brow. He had dropped out of school early, rarely found and never kept a job. He moved like a shadow among us.

When Morris was having one of his headaches quiet was enforced in the house. This meant that we could not play the phonograph. That was a deprivation. The phonograph was the thing about that house that Frankie and I loved most. Abe Klein spent on records more than he could afford. Mostly singers—Caruso, Galli Curci, Pasquale Amato, John McCormick; and the Russian favorites—Chaliapin, Rosa Raizen; but also fiddlers— Mischa Elman and Kreisler. Young Heifetz (possessively called Yahschalih Chaifitzle) was then thrilling the world with the most perfect fiddling of which man could be capable. I can't remember whether his records were then available. If they were, Abe Klein had them.

Many, many years later I worked in North Jersey. Daily I did a commute to Long Island. Once, returning from work, I saw Morris Klein leave the Jersey train I had been on and walk a space in Penn Station. He had not changed a bit. He looked the same. He walked the same way, head down, oblivious to everything around him. Had he, I wondered, at last found a job? If so, I was glad.

When I was about ten, Frankie Klein was about fourteen, already out of public school. When he worked he was off early and back late, always with a book under his arm. Often he was without a job and during summers had time to lounge on his stoop and read or chat.

Frankie was very short and broad-shouldered. He had a large, prominent, hooked nose. His chin was long, jutted forward and moved very interestingly when he spoke. His brow was high and his sandy hair long. The early beginnings of baldness made his brow even higher and, together with his other attributes, helped to give one the impression that here was a brain.

These other attributes included an accent unusual for the Bronx. He articulated carefully, his vowels were clean, his consonants crisp and his speech ran to the bookish. Since he was utterly innocent and sincere, social and completely tolerant (even of me, four enormous years his junior) he was well liked by the kids. Older people thought him an oddball. When we were not otherwise engaged we kids clustered about him, listened when he spoke and were perfectly willing to hear about Socrates, Michelangelo, Tchaikovsky, Heine or even Marcus Aurelius. Month by month, step by step, as I thought and read, I was able to follow Frankie further and further into this luminous world.

The other distinguishing attribute of Frankie was his

devotion to art. He drew, he painted (as well as possible in a crowded tenement flat, and often outdoors) and he visited museums. At a very early age I would (without anyone's consent) go with him to the Metropolitan Museum of Art. We went and sometimes returned without spending the nickel fare. The trick was as follows. Several miles from where we lived there was a junction point between the elevated train and the subway. People wishing to switch from one to the other were issued "transfers." Often people took transfer slips without intending to change trains. They would drop the slips on the stairs or in the street. We would pick them up, ride down to 86th Street and Lexington Avenue and visit the museum.

With awe and reverence we climbed the long flight to the second floor, our eyes on Raphael's Madonna altarpiece as it came into view above us, inch by inch. Then we stood before it. Religious? Yes! But an easy-going, undemanding religion. Innocent? Yes! But the innocence of a very pretty girl of this world. Color? It caressed the eye and murmured of pleasure to the soul. More secular and more exciting to look at, was a large Veronese on the wall facing the Raphael. It was a "Mars and Venus." On the lap of the muscular, bearded God sat a very naked Venus looking down at an impish, winged little Cupid, squirting a jet of milk at him from her pink nipple.

Hour after hour we wandered through the galleries, adoring, studying, envying. Frankie's tastes were much more cultivated than mine.

I admired the showy (Bonheur, Tiepolo, Caravaggio), the slick (David, Ingres), the campy (*The Storm, Pygmalion and Galatea*). Frankie taught me to look at Rembrandt's painting of light and the miracle of his brush strokes, at Monet's shimmering Rouen Cathedral, at Van Eyck's sound and simple structures under the meticulous detail.

How often we went I don't recall. But from then on I could tell you what painting hung on almost every wall of every gallery. I can, to this day, close my eyes, see whole walls of paintings and see as though standing before it, every painting on the wall.

How distressed I was, in later years, at the succession of changes which moved paintings and removed many to the cellar; and how glad to see some of the old ones come back.

How did we get home? I might volunteer to tell a policeman that we had lost our money. Sometimes we hitched rides uptown and would walk miles from where we were dropped. I remember once we hopped on the rear step of a horse-drawn ice wagon and rode from about 100th Street clear across the Willis Avenue Bridge into the Bronx.

Anything else Frankie might have done with his mind was foreclosed by his intense desire to become an artist. His talent was real and good. We often painted and drew together near the Bronx River or on the tenement rooftops. He admired my quick slap dashing (by contrast with his painstaking realism). But he was far better, and certainly more conscientious than I. I still have a conté crayon drawing he did of an early girlfriend of mine. The resemblance is remarkable and the drawing is good—crisp, free and fresh.

Frankie labored to produce a portfolio of work in the hope of finding a job as a commercial artist. He would clip the want ads for commercial artists and trek downtown with his portfolio. It was hopeless. Frankie was merely good. He had none of the fakery that passed for "style" and his very presence must have made people in the commercial studios either laugh or cry.

So, evenings he would return, depressed, and hole up for a day or two. I told him often that the worst thing he could do to himself as an artist was to work in a commercial art shop; that his best bet was to get a night job and paint and draw during the day. He was stubborn and immune. He continued to pursue his frustrations. And so Heine and Marcus Aurelius slowly faded into the shadows of his disappointments and anger.

I did not then understand Frankie's hopeless tilting at windmills. Now I think I begin to understand. To take and hold any other kind of job would have pulled him away from the one activity that gave him joy and peace—the handling of a brush or pencil. He was not ruthless enough to sponge on his father for support while he pursued the pleasure of art. He was not confident enough to believe that he might, somehow, pursue that pleasure and manage to support himself as a fine artist. Even the pleasure itself had an edge of guilt—to give one's self up to it would be to yield to a form of hedonism foreign and inimical to the soul that came to him from countless generations of struggling, hard-working Jews. After all the only worthwhile reason for doing anything was to make something that had value. And the only way you could be sure it had value was through someone's willingness to pay for it. The apparent compromise of a job as a commercial artist may have been a mirage. But Frankie Klein could not, for these reasons, admit it.

Frankie never did become a commercial artist. He was, in the last days of our friendship, an upholsterer.

Years after the Fox Street period of our lives, and after a long gap in our contacts, I was invited to Frankie's wedding. It was in the girl's apartment, a small, modestly furnished place in the upper Bronx. Frankie was dressed in a dark suit and wore a sedate blue tie. On his head was a black homburg with a narrow, roll-edged brim, and in his lapel was a red carnation. The bride was dressed in a simple, wine-colored dress. She was shorter even than Frankie, plain of face and sweetly mannered. She was, for all I knew, Frankie's first woman.

I was unsettled by it—so different was it from any of the ambience I would have associated with Frankie. A flower-bedecked choopah (wedding bower) stood on the cleared floor. In a corner was an obsequious young Rabbi facing a cluster of people, nodding and smiling and raising his eyebrows and bobbing his head up and down. On one side was a long table set with a low-cost caterer's collation.

The ceremony was orthodox, and at last I saw my friend Frankie, the agnostic, the ranging mind, the hungry soul, crush the wrapped wine glass with his heel. So badly was I unbalanced by the event that I went up to Frankie's mother and said, "Mrs. Klein! You are not losing a son; you are gaining a daughter!" I still crawl at the memory of my banality.

THE HEROES

Sammy Raden

Sammy lived on 156th Street. He was about two years older than l, and while I was still in public school, had already gone out into the big world. I believe, in fact, that he never got to eighth grade but left through some special dispensation.

Sammy was handsome and well built, bright and adventurous. He was broad-shouldered and flat-bellied and, even when quite young, fully and markedly musculated. He had curly black hair, bright eyes, a short round nose and a cleft chin. He was the most frequent organizer of walks to Barretto Point and the best swimmer on the block. He had begun to sprout pubic hair when the rest of us were still smooth-skinned all the way down. And so, while we went naked off the pier he would wear a black bikini type of jock.

The rest of us would jump in, holding our noses, splashing about in a dog paddle. Sammy dove cleanly and swam with both arms overhand, his palms making flat slaps on the water and pulling him leisurely forward. A good distance off in the East River was a garbage-dumping island. While we splashed about, never far from the wooden cleats that formed a ladder at the end of the pier, Sammy would set straight out with his leisurely paddle for Garbage Island. Soon we would all be back on the pier watching him getting smaller and smaller in the distance, until even the wavelet nipples of the river were enough to hide his head. We would see him, a small speck, get onto the Island, mount a rock and dive back.

He ruled us, in these excursions, with easy grace. He decided on my first trip to the Point with the gang that I would learn how to swim. He simply ordered that I be grabbed, shoulder and ankles, and flung over the side. Since the water was about twenty feet deep at the jetty's end, it was sink or swim for me. I was a struggling piece of jetsam among orange rinds, goldfish (human feces) and scumbags (condoms) engaged in enough of a compromise between sinking and swimming to get me back to the ladder. For this I admired Sammy even more.

The roofs of the tenements stretching along 156th between Fox and Southern Boulevard were a favorite gathering place. Since the roofs were joined by meeting sidewalls, it was easy to fraternize. A favorite meeting place was the pigeon coop several roofs down from Fox.

Sammy came up to the roof one summer afternoon while I was leaning against the parapet watching the birds. It was a custom for the bird owners to send their birds out when a stray pigeon was flying about, hoping that it would join the flock and return with them. The boys had long bamboo poles with a piece of red rag tied at the end and they would wave these at the flock, to keep it in flight, swerving around and around.

Sammy sat next to me, watching. While most of the birds were out several were still in the coop. Sammy pointed to a group of three. One was crouched in a corner, watching the other two. Of these one was a male, fat in an enormous pout, strutting and bobbing about the other, a slender female who pretended not to notice him but picked delicately at the grain on the floor of the coop.

"See that?" said Sammy. "The one in the corner is the fat one's wife. The skinny one is cherry. (This was vernacular for "virgin," referring to the hymen.) Pigeons stay married. But if the male can grab a piece of cherry— goodbye Charlie! Say, Natie, have you gotten your hump yet? No! I'll take you sometime. Where? Well, there's this woman. She's a Negro, but she's real clean. Before she lets you, she takes a clean rag and wipes herself out. You don't want? OK. It's up to you!"

Sammy once persuaded me to go with him to a theatre near the junction of Third and Westchester Avenues, a far walk, where "high grade" vaudeville acts were put on. I didn't care much for the loud, unrelenting brassy music and the struggling, sweating actors. But Sammy was entranced. One of the artists was a singer with a very low cut sequined gown and enormous earrings, who belted out ballads while garish lights were played on her. Sammy wriggled and made admiring clucks while she flung at us: "If you can't tell the woild she's a good little goil, then just say nothing at all..."

Sammy's applause was wild and long. After it he turned to me. "Don't think she's just a bum," he said of the singer. "I know her. She's a good girl. She brings home her pay to her mother."

Tommy Riordan

The Riordans lived on the top floor of our tenement. Mr. Riordan was a tall, quiet, square-faced man. He worked "for the subway." I think he was a track walker.

111

He is sharpest in my memory as a dark figure trudging up 156th Street on the way home from work with the evening sky behind him. His clothes grimy, his face and hands smeared with soot and grease, a lunch box hanging from his arm, he was like a looming, sad golem.

There were two Riordan boys. The older began to work for the subway some years after we moved to Fox Street. Then there would be a smaller silhouette trudging by Mr. Riordan's side up 156th.

Tommy was my age—blond, blue-eyed, quick and witty. He would walk along the curb, one foot on the curbstone, the other in the gutter, singing in a lilt:

Oh pity me! Pity me! Pity me do!
I was bahrn on the soid of a hill!

He could say "born" and "side" with the rest of us.

Tommy would join us Jewish kids when a Springhurst gang raid was taking place and he was the most fearless of us, organizing and deploying us.

Tommy left school early to go to work. And soon he was trudging up 156th street on dark evenings with his brother and his father.

On Sundays Tommy Riordan was washed and clean and would hang out with us at the newspaper stand in front of the candy store. As a workingman Tommy would dominate the group. He would jingle coins in his pocket and sometimes gave a penny to a wide-eyed kid hovering about him. "Go buy yourself a bellyache," he would say.

When I was a kid I used to dream of finding money. There would be shiny coins at my feet and I would follow their trail, picking them up until they were heavy in my pockets and flowed out of my hands; and there were always more and more. One day I said to Tommy, "Isn't it wonderful to be grown up and have money in your pocket all the time, so you can buy what you want without asking anybody?"

Tommy snorted and said, "Yeah, and be picking Indian Nuts out of your ass-hole hair!"

Indian Nuts were small brown roundish nuts with buttery kernels. They were dispensed from penny slot machines in front of the candy store. Together with sunflower seeds, usually dispensed from another glass-bowl slot machine, they were a favorite ky-shpy (chew and spit). Tommy's reference was to the fecal nodules that adhered between the buttocks of an incompletely wiped behind. Ever since that day my image of maturity has had Tommy Riordan's aphorism hanging from its neck.

Al Singer

All boxing fans know this name. Singer became one of the great lightweights of all time. He was not much older than the rest of us, but already dedicated to boxing as a career. He was made for it. He was taciturn and grim. There was challenge and menace in his very walk and in his lowered head and side-glancing eyes. Mr. and Mrs. Singer ran the candy store in our building. Glossy photos of Al, his gloves raised, his eyes fixed on you, his face set, were all over the place. You couldn't buy a glass of seltzer without hearing about their darling Alickle. They assumed that he was the king and pride of the neighborhood and that you would, merely because of that fact, patronize the Singers' candy store. It wasn't always so.

Singer had a younger sister going to public school the same time as we did. She was big, developing an early bust and sharing the domineering attitude of the rest of the Singers. She spouted scandal, copiously and indiscriminately. She would posit endless and impossible liaisons; between every female teacher in P.S. 52 and every male—from gym teachers all the way up to the principal. There was a harmless old Irish lady teacher whom she *knew* to be a "dope fiend." How? Because the smell of mint in her room after lunch was obviously meant to hide the smell of dope. Not even my beloved Miss Schwartz was spared.

I detested this girl. Once, after she left the stoop smelling of her foul mouth, I said to the others, "That's some slut!"

Very soon after, Al Singer appeared at the base of the stoop and looked up at me. "C'mon down here," he said. I obeyed. "You insulted my sister. Put your hands up." Before I completed making a gesture of expostulation, I was smashed in the mid-riff, doubled over and falling through a pit of dark, pulsing colors and searing pain.

I never had any revenge lust against the Springhurst kids. But after writing the above paragraph I had a waking fantasy in which Singer was matched with an opponent who outdanced and outweighted him, got Singer to throw a right at the wrong time and then floored him with a crushing uppercut to the chin.

THE DUDS

Galahad

There was a man on the block, Mr. Asher, who was politically anonymous, smiled and nodded at everybody, though he sought no one's friendship and never participated in any of the fruit box klatches. He was a union official. He had a son our age, Sollie, who often tried to join us in our play. Sollie was neither athletic nor graceful and we had the feeling, later confirmed, that he was not quite satisfied with our games. Within a short time we discovered why. He was reading about King Arthur and the Knights of the Round Table. He gobbled up their tales of bravery and adventure. His idea was that we should play King Arthur games. Slay dragons and rescue maidens. We looked at him with surprise. "King Arthur? Gahwahn!"

The books that most moved us were: a) The various colored "fairy tale" books (the Green, Red, Blue, etc. Fairy Tale Books), which we consumed on the sly. Sometimes you would discover one lying about another kid's house. If he knew you saw it he would say, "That's the sissy stuff my sister reads." Once in a rare while two kids would confess to each other their addiction and avidly compare notes about the tales of frogs that were princes, maidens put to deep sleep by wicked witches, and so on. This was an honored secret. You never told anyone that your friend read fairy tales. You were, after all, vulnerable too. b) The Frank Merriwell books. These dealt with an incredible Yale man who was the best athlete, the best detective, the bravest adventurer, the cleanest liver and the most persistent do-gooder of all time. They were read openly and avidly and were actively traded. A kid with a stock of Frank Merriwell books that you hadn't read was someone to cultivate. Usually he had read all of yours and you needed money or an item for barter. I once gave away a pushmobile for fifteen Frank Merriwells.

(A note for the uninitiated: Wherever construction is taking place there are odd lengths of 2 by 4 lumber lying about. Wherever there are skates, one gets lost. Wherever there is a fruit store there is a fruit box, begged from the fruit man or pinched from a grown-up who has risen from hers to chase her brat or buy a "glagzle seltzer." These were the main ingredients of a pushmobile. At the ends of a two to three foot length of 2 x 4 you nailed the front and back sections of a skate, obtained by loosening the nut that held them together. At the front end you nailed a fruit box, hollow side facing rear, bottom facing front. To the top of the fruit box you nailed two sticks, jutting out diagonally, to act as "steerers." If your skate wheels were of the preferred "bail berrian" variety—i.e. with ball bearings, instead of the clunky learner type—you had an efficient vehicle. You put one foot on the 2 x 4, hands on the steerer, and pushed with the other foot. On smooth asphalt or downhill one push sent you a long distance. Then you could put both feet on and feel the wind against your cheeks and in your hair).

One of the memorable experiences of my life was looking at the front covers of the limp, page-shedding volumes for which I had traded my pushmobile. Each had a lurid picture of Frank Merriwell doing his stuff—holding off a gang of girl-molesters, looking slant eyed at the man on first as he was about to pitch the last out of the crucial Yale-Harvard game, rising from a card table to denounce a cheat, knocking a whiskey glass from a friend's hand, etc., etc. Here were hours and hours of absorption and excitement to come.

None of this reading was reflected in our games: the fairy books for obvious reasons and the Frank Merriwells (or Tom Swifts or Rover Boys or Horatio Algers) because they were too complex, too unreal and—while primitive—weren't primal enough to yield kid's games.

Well, to get back to Sollie Asher. We were more than cold—we were downright contemptuous of his suggestions. How could they compare with cops and robbers, cowboys and Indians, king of the hill, stickball?

There came a time, however, when Sollie had his day. The Saturday movie at the Empire was one in which King Arthur's knights joined in a battle against the wicked Saracens during a Crusade. That gave us something to imitate. We had garbage pail covers for shields and our swords were pointed lengths of lathing, with short crosspieces as hand guards. The enemy was identifiable and hateful; so hateful that only by requiring every kid to take a turn at being a wicked Saracen could we muster up a battle.

Sollie's day was a short one. Very soon after, a Doug Fairbanks movie appeared and we abandoned swords for ropes to tie to the bottom slats of the first floor fire escapes so that we could swing out and land, clomp, on our hands and knees.

Nightscheh and Frood

Almost as soon as I was old enough to get there by myself I would walk the goodly number of blocks between Fox Street and the Woodstock branch of the public Library. Set in a noisy, littered, crowded market street, it was a dignified structure of heavy granite blocks. It had high, deep windows and iron door lamps which sprouted tiaras of long, gracefully bent spikes. You left this world when you entered the place and stepped on the clean cork floor, ran your hand on the polished oak front desk, bathed in the quiet—the heavenly quiet—and smelled the books. You came with clean hands because the "lyberrian" insisted on inspecting them before you passed the front desk.

Once in, I would wander before the shelves, pull out books at random and bring them to a table. *Animals of the Western World*, *How to Build Bird Houses*, *A Handbook of Small Arms*—these were for the pictures. Progressively my reading went from the fairy tales to Jack London, Maupassant, Poe and Shaw, and books on the body and mind: G. Stanley Hall's *Adolescence*, William James' *The Varieties of Religious Experience*, Freud's *The Interpretation of Dreams*, or *The Lazy Colon*, a junk book about constipation whose title fascinated me and will always live in my memory. I read avidly about the lives of painters and sculptors and, having heard these names mentioned by Frank Klein, I struggled as best I could with Nietzsche, Spengler, Plato, and Marcus Aurelius.

As this reading progressed I migrated from the front of Fox Street to the front of Frankie Klein's house and to the roofs. Physical play gave way to talk—rarely political, but about books, ideas, or people.

Two duds are associated with this period; Al Margolies and Gisella Tarsh.

Al Margolies was a hanger-on at conversations. He was insecure and by turns aggressive and humble. He was an early public school dropout who described his job as "communications." We found out later from his kid brother that he worked as a WUT—a Western Union telegram deliverer. Al Margolies never began or contributed to a topic of conversation. In a truculent mood he would lean against the side of the stoop, his arms folded across his chest, his eyebrows knit, and from time to time he would burst out with a sarcastic comment or criticism. "That's for suckers to believe!" or "You read Marcus Aurelius? Tell that to the Marines!"

Al Margolies' humble moods would come on him sometimes when he was alone with me. Once while I was on the roof, watching the pigeons, he joined me to talk. What were Nightscheh and Frood really all about? Those who know me will not be at all surprised to hear that I proceeded coincidently and unhesitatingly, to give an answer. I didn't correct his pronunciation overtly but made sure to speak the names Neet-shee and Froyd very distinctly. While I talked he listened, head down, his elbows on his knees, rolling a piece of roof pitch in his fingers. When I finished he sat quietly, looked up at the sky for a while and then rose and walked off.

I thought that something I had said hurt or offended him. Since he was several years older than I it was, in the ethics of my time, a very bad thing to do. By the time I rose to follow him the sheet metal door of the roof entrance had been slammed shut by the weight on the pulley and he had already clomped down several flights of steps.

The Nafkih

Two sisters lived in Frankie Klein's building. One was Flora Tarsch, slightly older than we, who would sometimes grace us patronizingly with her presence. She worked at the ticket booth of a nearby movie house and as was customary in her profession, wore heavy make-up and "fancy" clothes. She had the "aura" of theatre about her and she knew it. She gossiped about the movie stars of the day as though they were her intimates and once hinted that she might be offered a chance to go to Hollywood herself.

Flora Tarsch's older sister was Gisella. Until Flora told us more about her, all we knew about her was her name and her appearance. She was short, had a small white face with round eyes over which her lids drooped in a slant—so that she always looked sleepy. She had bleached hair, which straggled out from under a knit hat, pulled down on her head and circled with a folded up band. She had virtually no lips—but a crease formed by the infolding of her mouth. Her chin jutted slightly forward as do the chins of toothless people. Her legs were stumpy, her ankles of approximately the same diameter as her calves. She wore heavy cloth or fur coats with long sleeves. She would walk with her arms folded under her bosom, her hands hidden by her sleeves, plodding slowly, each shoulder rising and falling with her steps. She never spoke, even when passing her sister on the stoop.

Once, after passing Flora on the way in, Gisella paused at the entrance and turned her head to give us all a look of tired contempt.

When she was well in, Flora nodded backwards and said: "She's a hoor. She works over a store on twenty-eight street. She takes kids. Any of you that wants can have her upstairs anytime my mother isn't home."

None of us was tempted.

KADISCH FOR A GOY

To this day more than fifty years later, Anton Kubin weighs on my conscience. When I think about him the thoughts are tender. I knew his name before I knew him. He occupied a street floor apartment on 156th Street and his window carried a low, narrow sign. "Anton Kubin—Violin Lessons, Sales, Repairs and Sundries."

From my earliest days on Fox Street that window attracted me. In the summer the window would be open and Mr. Kubin would sit there, scraping violin tops or backs with pieces of broken glass, his window sign over his head.

He was a lean man with a true Prussian face and head. His iron-grey hair was always close-cropped. The back of his neck rose straight to the top of his head, without meeting a prominence at the back of his skull. He had small grey eyes which were luridly enlarged by the strong lenses of his gold-rimmed glasses. His eyebrows were bushy and clipped. His slight jowls creased straight down on either side of a prominent dimpled chin.

During World War I Mr. Kubin was a frequent victim of the anti-German fever. His windows were smashed several times. The kids soon forgot this, but Mr. Kubin did not. He would not tolerate their loitering on the stoop or at the cellar rail under his window. He would shoo me off with the rest. But I would merely back off and keep watching.

He came to tolerate me. One day, after my violin lessons with Mr. Sentner began, while I was lolling on the stoop watching him, I blurted, "I'm taking violin" (swinging a leg over the stoop railing and back). He gave no acknowledgement, but rose, disappeared and soon came back with some coins. He said, "Go to Marshall's and buy two rolls and a quarter pound limburger." His accent was recognizably, but not markedly, German.

When I returned he beckoned me to come to his door; it opened on the ground floor hallway. He met me at the door, a tall figure with very bowed legs. "Come in." He walked ahead of me in a narrow corridor that had an open toilet door facing the main door and that led to the front room on one side and the kitchen on the other. He led me to the kitchen, sat me down, opened the bag I had brought, broke off a piece of roll, smeared a generous glob of limburger on it and handed it to me.

"Eat." The cheese had the powerful smell of a freshly and plentifully used outhouse.

I did not want to offend him by refusing. I ate, with the same feeling I had when I was thrown off the pier at Barretto Point. I survived, and then and there acquired a taste for stinky cheeses. He nodded approvingly and himself chewed away with the slow jaw motions of a man with ill-fitting dentures.

One look and one smell of the dark disordered kitchen and of the unmade bed in a dark bedroom beyond it made it clear that the reason I had never seen a Mrs. Kubin was that there wasn't one. I was glad to follow him to the front room, lit by the two windows facing the street.

Mr. Kubin walked stiffly and made grimaces when he sat or rose. He never talked of ailments. But I realized many years later, when I recalled him, that he must have lived in constant pain from widespread arthritis.

When he reached the front room he took a hanging fiddle and bow from the wall, made scraping attacks on the strings to tune them and handed the instrument and stick to me.

"Play."

I made a bad imitation of bravura fingering and bowing. He was expressionless. He reached for the fiddle and bow and hung them back on the wall.

Mr. Kubin's front room had a large table covered with an old tapestry-weave cloth. The table was littered with fiddle parts and fiddlemaker's tools. Set against a wall was an old upright piano with crazed varnish and uneven keys. Above the piano hung a large mezzotint of Richard Wagner. A Morris chair, with cracked leather seat and back, filled one corner. Violins in various states of completion, bows, bow-sticks and bow-hair hung on the walls. There were cabinets with small drawers filled with bridges, mutes, tailpieces, chin-rests, fine tuners, pegs. Every horizontal surface of this room was filled with fiddle litter or with old "Staats-Zeitung" newspapers or books or empty tobacco cans. There was always a pipe dangling from Mr. Kubin's mouth and he and this room bore the pungent odor of pipe tobacco.

My visits were repeated again and again for the next six or seven years. The scope of our relationship and of my errands for him increased. My violin playing improved. There came a time when he said, "More!"

I would play chess with him—almost invariably losing. If a game developed to my advantage, Mr. Kubin would knit his brows and look closely at the pieces for a long time, as though trying to discover which one of his had gone over to the other side, or had otherwise betrayed him.

It became a ritual for me to bring to him, before sitting down to my own Friday night supper, a small pot of chicken soup with noodles and boiled chicken that was being cooked for our meal at home.

I would give him haircuts. The clippers made a sharp crackling noise as they went through his stiff hair. He explained that as you got older the silicon content of your hair and nails increased.

I would make trips to the Library for him. He was a discriminating reader. He read through all of Thomas Hardy and Ibsen as well as the contemporary German novelists (in English).

Mr. Kubin never left his apartment. I never knew or asked how he supported himself. I never saw a pupil; I never saw a customer. To my knowledge only one other person ever visited him. That was a short, thin dark man who came once in a while with a bag of groceries. I was never introduced to him. When he came I was hustled out.

Very soon after I entered high school my range began to extend far beyond Fox Street and I visited Mr. Kubin less often. One day as I was passing in front of his building I noticed that his sign was gone and his walls were bare. I knocked at his door. The little, dark man answered and let me in. He was sweeping. The furniture was gone and packages were heaped on the floor.

"What happened?"

"Mr. Kubin moved to Simpson Street. Here, he said to give you the address. He wants to see you."

Although Simpson Street was an easy walk, I did not go.

About a year later I met the little, dark man on the street .

He looked at me resentfully. He said.

"You were very cruel to him. He liked you. He needed you and you didn't go to see him. He wanted to give you his violins."

"He's dead?"

"Yes."

"Did he have any family?"

"Only a sister in Poland."

"Poland?"

"Yes. He was Polish."

By the world's reckoning Mr. Kubin did nothing for me. Yet I remember him with great tenderness and my conscience hurts for having abandoned him. I intend what I wrote here as my Kadisch for him.

LIFE IN COMMERCE

The Odd Jobs

Beginning quite early—I would guess at about ten—I took after-school jobs. Mostly these were held sub-rosa, when I was supposed to be in Chayder. I remember only a few.

The Laundry: A small retail laundry on Southern Boulevard. The owner was a short, quickly moving hustler. My job was to pick up from customers (loading the bags in a push truck on noisy iron wheels), sort laundry (shaking out roaches) and making deliveries. What I remember most were the tea-drinking sessions my boss had in the back of the store with a neighboring storekeeper. Their conversation was basic. "Ich kenn ah shaynih nafkalih. Villst eintinken a bissel?" "Ver darrf. Ahz mi trent ah mool mit a customer izz ginnig." (I know a nice little whore. Would you like to dip in a bit? Who needs it. If you screw once in a while with a customer it's enough.)

I was found out by my mother and forced to leave this job and return to Chayder. My boss urged me to come back with the promise that if I did he would let me know which of my lady customers would be willing to show me the ropes. I never went back.

The Florist: Also on Southern Boulevard. My job was to make deliveries. It was not a very active place. To keep myself busy I would cut out small cards and indite on them, in the fanciest calligraphy I could manage, such inspired and stimulating slogans as "Our Motto: Quality and Service" or "The Boulevard Florist For all your Floral Needs," etc. My boss, a practical and dyspeptic man, would look sourly at my creations. Before long I was fired. I am sure my saccharine signs helped him to a decision. I didn't mind. I hated the smell of roses.

Sachet Powder: I once clipped an ad from one of the kids' magazines: "Win this gorgeous bike or this Daisy BB gun. Just sell packets of our delicious sachet powder and win one of these terrific prizes…"

I duly mailed back the coupon and before long received in the mail a cardboard box with small envelopes of perfumed powders. There were about six different varieties—Rose, Honeysuckle, Trailing Arbutus, etc. They were to sell at 10¢ per packet. I sold one to my mother and after school on the next day I trudged block after block, stopping where the women sat and gossiped, or rocked baby carriages. I hawked "Satshit powders; Roses, Trailing Arubttis," etc. I found no takers. But a lady with a kind face said, "Show me what you have there, boy." I did. "That," she said, "is *Sashay* powder. And this," holding up a packet, "is Trailing *Arbeautous*." She didn't buy any.

I then tried a disgusting ploy. I limped slightly. It wasn't hard. I had walked a long way. I called my "Sashay powders" in a plaintive voice. It didn't help. In hours of traipsing I sold two packets and the box weighed like lead on my sad trudge home. I put the box into a drawer and forgot about the powders. But I did not forget about the BB rifle on which my heart had been set. For several nights I sat listlessly at supper, pottskying (dabbling) with my food. My father asked my mother, "vooss izz

130

mittim kint?" (What's with the kid?) She explained. A few days later I woke to find a long cardboard box lying next to me on the bed.

Weeks went by. Then I got a letter:

"Dear Cooperator: It has been some time since we heard from you. Please report to us on your progress. If you have sold any of the packets send us the money either in coins or stamps."

I ignored this letter. Then another:

"Dear Cooperator: We did not think you were the type to ignore our last letter. This is a reminder that we wish to hear from you and receive payment for merchandise which you do not return."

Then another:

"Dear Sir: Unless we hear from you to our satisfaction within ten days we will submit this matter to our counsel for appropriate legal action."

That was the last of the letters. The sachet powders lay in the drawer for a long time. They were loose. I had taken the box to house an ill-matched chess set I bought from another kid, who delivered the pieces in an old sock.

Later I discovered that the roses, honeysuckles, trailing arbutuses and what-nots, all had the same smell.

Jelly Apples: I had an aunt, "Tante Meyer" who visited us very seldom. Tante Meyer was reputed to be "oongeshtuft" (stuffed) with jewelry, bought with all the Meyer savings. She was short, very fat, with a head of abundant black hair and slanted, dark, kohl-lined eyes. She wore low cut dresses of shiny material and her short fat fingers and pudgy wrists were crusted with rings and bracelets. There was an electric aura around her. Her husband, tall, fat, florid, owned restaurants. One was on Rivington Street in the lower East Side. Sometimes my father took me down there and we ate Roumanian food to our heart's content. On one of these trips my father took me for a ride on a horse drawn trolley. I think the trolley ran on Delancey Street.

Tante Meyer was the cause of some grief to my brother. The grief came when Tante Meyer died, years later. She had married, after the death of her restaurant owner husband and shortly before her own death, a devout blood-sucking Jew who pawned everything of hers he could lay his hands on. Tante Meyer made a will excluding him and naming my older brother as executor and chief legatee. When my brother dug her vaunted jewels out of the vault he found only a few tawdry pieces left. A friend of his was a jeweler. The friend appraised the jewels for my brother and bought them for the appraised price. The bloodsucker hired a lawyer, claimed a right to the estate and sued my brother for a surcharge for having defrauded the estate. It was an expensive settlement.

Where was I? Yes! Jelly apples. One of Uncle Meyer's ventures was a small hot dog booth on the Rockaway Boardwalk. My father persuaded him to make and sell jelly apples. As a beginning my father brought down a large bag of apples, some stick sugar and red vegetable dye. He boiled the sugar in water, mixed in the red coloring, stuck sticks into the apples, dipped them into the syrup and set them out on a tray lined with waxed paper. The apples dripped a flat base for themselves. Then I was given a pocket full of change and sent out on the beach to peddle the apples at 10¢ each. I was doing very well. In about ten minutes half my tray of apples was gone.

But then a large figure loomed over me. It was a policeman with a billy (truncheon). "Hey kid! Do you have a peddler's license? No...? Then get the hell out of here and don't let me catch you again!"

On my way back I saw a toddler vainly trying to brush sand from his jelly apple. I gave him a fresh one.

Thus ended the jelly apple venture.

Jelly Donuts: Some fate kept steering my jobs to Southern Boulevard. When I was about eleven my father did one of his disappearing acts. His last store, like every other one he had, failed. He had not enough to start a new one. My mother, who was perennially tearing money from him as a vulture tears at a carcass, would not give him a cent—it was for my older brother's education. There was a fight—one of many. They roared themselves hoarse. My mother clawed at my father. He grasped a kitchen knife and came toward her. She retreated to the stove and threw at his head a pot of hot melted fat that was being rendered. He had a red blotch on his bald head for years after. The kitchen table was thrown over; people above us banged on their floor; people below hit their ceiling with a broomstick; windows slammed open all around the air-shift; people yelled: Sharrap awready! Zeit shtill! Facrissake stop! Call a cop!"

I ran out of the house in terror and walked the streets, not seeing or hearing anything, plodding through a misery never equaled in my grown-up years. I had run from fights many times before and, I imagine, this variety of misery was cumulative. I did not go home. Instead I went to my sister's apartment and asked to sleep there. A cot was set up for me in the corridor of her apartment.

Early next morning my mother came, said my father had gone, and told me to come home. I refused. I went to school without my books. I came back to my sister's for lunch and found her out, wheeling her baby. I realized that I could not expect her to make lunch for me or give me an allowance. So I looked for and found a job—in the building next to my sister's apartment.

In a small store, with a single counter and rack of shelves, a slender, sour-faced man made and sold donuts and crullers. In the back of the shop he kneaded and shaped the dough and dropped the pieces into a large vat of hot fat. They would sink, rise, give off a halo of bubbles and soon turn brown. The donuts were set on trays and pumped with jelly from a large syringe with a pointed nozzle.

He needed a boy to make deliveries. Certain customers had standing orders for breakfast crullers or donuts. These had to be delivered very early. And so I would get up at about 5:30, pull my clothes from under the cot, dress quickly, drink a glass of milk and hurry to the job. Sometimes I found the bags, each marked with an address and apartment number, ready for me. Sometimes I helped to bag and mark. Then I would carry the oily bags around the neighborhood in a large basket, leaving them in front of apartment doors and walking off after two sharp knocks at the door.

When I first took the job I looked forward to feasts on fresh jelly donuts. After a while I would no more bite into one than I would into a lump of putty.

The Sunday Shoot

I invented a game and made money at it. It was played on Sunday because that was when the working-men would stand around with nothing to do and they were needed to make the game worthwhile. You have to understand a little of the geography. Directly in front of 744 Fox was a hill out of which the street had been cut. On that hill was "The Martinique Mansion," a stuccoed building owned by a caterer and at which neighborhood weddings, bar mitzvahs and other functions were held. The face of the hill directly across from us was mostly sandstone ledge that had been blasted down. This rock had many crevices and projections.

I had the Daisy BB rifle which I did not earn by selling "sashay" powder, and was an extraordinarily good shot. I would put a bottle or can or card up on a projection of the hill stone and, from the curb in front of our building, aim at it. Someone was always watching. One Sunday one of the men asked, "Noo, Mr. Mocksmin, you think you can hit a dime?" I said I'd try. I hit the dime he put up and he let me keep it. Other men became interested and, for a turn with the gun, each put a dime up on the rock. Whoever hit a dime got it. Since my rifle and BBs were being used I got a free turn. Many, many were the dimes I shot down.

Schlivovitz

My father was a moonshiner in a very modest way. During prohibition he would ferment a barrel of prunes in a large wooden vat in the bathroom and distill a prune brandy (schlivovitz) in a still set in the bathtub. He ran a long rubber tube from the bathroom gas light fixture to a small, single burner under the still and cooked the mash. From another pipe attached to a water tap he had a steady stream of cold water running down the coils to condense the alcohol. This came out in small drips, running through a filter-paper lined funnel into a gallon glass jug. The liquid came out water-clear. My father would heat dry sugar in a small pan until it melted and turned brown. Then he would add a little water, pour the result into the gallon jug, shake it and produce a pleasant golden color in the schlivovitz. It was, apparently, good liquor. He had many customers who came to the apartment with milk bottles to be filled with the stuff.

He continued to produce this brandy while I was in high school. Then when some friends and I would have all-night picnics at Pelham Bay Park, some would bring salami, some bread, some scallions and I would bring brandy poured from one of my father's gallon jugs. I would always pour back a measure of water equal to the measure of brandy I took. Since my father didn't drink he never noticed the difference. Apparently his customers didn't either.

THE WAR AND I

America entered World War I a year after we moved to Fox Street. Except for a few wounds to my young soul the War just brushed by me. There were no bands, no parades, no recruiting speeches. I don't recall seeing a single soldier in uniform on the block.

My first intense experience with the War came from some of the older kids on the block. The noisier, rowdier, and more athletic ones among them tended to be the most patriotic. At the height of the anti-German fever they would gossip in low, menacing voices about various families, almost all Jewish, accusing them of being "Pro-German." "Let's get that Maxie, his old man is Pro-German!" "Let's break Dr. Bach's windows, he's Pro-German!" About poor Mr. Kubin, whose windows were smashed several times, there was no doubt, "He was a "German spy!"

There was a look in their eyes that was new and disturbing to me. They were no longer Fox Street kids. They were a mob lusting for violence. Long after the fever and the War had gone I remembered this about them. And those that had been the incendiaries for that short time were never the same to me again.

A life-long dislike for my brother-in-law Al began during the War. Al was my mother's idol. He had alleh myeliss (all the virtues). He was tall. He was born in this country. He had a job as a "saylissmahn." His father was a department store floorwalker with a slick, polite manner. For a while after their marriage Al and my sister lived with us at

Fox Street. This was one of the few periods of our life in that apartment when the round oak table of the dining-living room was used for eating, rather than as a place on which to dump and leave whatever anyone wanted to put down. We were too many to fit around the kitchen table.

We were seated at the dining room table one Friday evening having the traditional soup with noodles and boiled chicken. My brother-in-law, as usual, lorded over the conversation. "The Germans are terrific fighters. Whatever they do, they do it better than anybody else. Their cannons are bigger and now they have aeroplanes that can drop bombs. Don't be surprised if one day soon we have German bombs dropping on us, vroom, just like that!"—with a downward thrust of his raised hands.

I listened, in fear, my imagination picturing for me the planes, the bombs, the explosions, the terror. At that very moment something heavy dropped onto the floor of the apartment above us, right over our heads. It made a big noise and rattled the colored glass dome of the gas light fixture, which hung above the table. My heart jumped. The awful thing had happened. The bombs were dropping. Apparently everyone else around the table had felt some of the fright—there was a long silence and loud laughter after the gaslight fixture stopped shaking.

I didn't laugh.

It was not until years later that I realized how vivid and menacing that remote War had been to me. We were cleaning out a bedroom closet. I came across an old geography book that had belonged to my brother and lay forgotten through the years toward the back of a high shelf in the closet.

The binding was hanging loose and a flyleaf page projected out. I saw some pencil marks at the edge of the flyleaf and flipped the cover back. The cover leaf and the facing leaf were filled with an elaborate and detailed drawing of a war scene I had made as a child. Foot soldiers were shooting and bayonetting each other. Bodies hung limp over barbed wire. Cannons on distant hills were puffing out smoke and their shells were coming to the scene in large arcs. Overhead, bi-planes were flying low, dropping bombs, dog fighting each other.

It was a child's drawing and any emotion—including pleasurable excitement—could have accompanied its making. But mine could not have been pleasurable excitement. The small faces of the soldiers showed hatred and agony. The limp corpses were the most carefully drawn and shaded of the figures. And if I needed any other hint how I felt when I made the drawing I gave it to myself when I stumbled on it. No emotion was recalled. But I flung the book down and walked from the room.

LEARNING, LEARNING, LEARNING

Music

Before hearing about my musical education you should know about music in P.S. 52. We were made to sing from a standard book apparently circulated among the city schools. Presumably the selections were based on someone's idea of what would be dear to our hearts for the rest of our days and in good taste. That someone chose such goodies as:

Far o'er the mountain
Ling'ring falls the southern moo-oon
There, o'er the fountain
Breaks the day too soo-oon.
Nita, Jua-ah-ah-nita,
Ask thy soul if we should pah-ahrt.
Nita, Jua-ah-ah-nita,
Lean thou on my hah-ahrt.

He was half right. This classic *will* remain with me for the rest of my days.

As a special treat we were occasionally visited by special teachers or invited guests. The special music teacher taught nothing. She performed. You could tell from the way she stood at the piano and talked, bosom big and head high, that music was a sacred thing. About all we learned from her was that our duty was to be a good audience, not picking our noses or rattling programs. After a summary of the place of an operatic aria in the ridiculous plot, she would seat herself at the piano, fidget into position and accompany herself. She would fling at us a vigorous and raspy, "Veesee dahrtay, vessee dahmoray..." or "Oon bell deeyih..."

How, after this woman, did any of us become reconciled to opera?

Introduced at "assembly" were such worthies as: Mr. Theremin who had invented and played an electronic instrument consisting of a box, with elaborate dials, from which projected vertically a rod like the antenna of a portable radio. He stood on a special mat and turned dials. As he did, a hum of varying pitch came out of the box. Having set the pitch, he played by gathering the fingers of one hand together, pointing them toward the rod and moving his hand back and forth with a vibrating motion. The nearer he came, the higher the pitch. The machine produced an obstinate, oscillating hum, without overtones or character.

And the Fiddle Juggler. Mr. Tricksy-Fiddle was an artist who came out with a victim, (his violin) a bow, a chair and a smile. He began by playing a few lovely bars of Bach's Air for the G string. I was enchanted. But soon he twirled his fiddle around, strings down, wrist up and bowed from underneath the scratch noises of a jig. Then he put the fiddle behind his neck and scratched out a few bars of a popular tune. This he continued with one foot up on the chair and the fiddle thrust under his thigh.

He carried it on, sitting on the chair, his bow held upright between his knees, his fiddle in his two hands, being rubbed up and down against the bow hairs. He ended by tossing his bow and fiddle high in the air and catching them deftly.

If Fox Street produced musicians or music-lovers it was despite P.S. 52. There *was* music on Fox Street. On a walk on a summer evening you would hear little girls at the piano playing scales or Beethoven's "Für Elise." You would hear little boys pulling out on their half or three-quarter size fiddles approximate scales or "La Cinquantaine." The phonographs would be going: Caruso, Cantor Rosenblatt, Galli Curci, Marche Slav.

Except for an accident, my older brother and I would have been piano players. My father bought for my brother and I imagine, eventually for me, an upright piano—on time, with a very small down payment. When the piano was delivered my mother had it placed in one of the bedrooms, so that it wouldn't get "tzihocked" (knocked about) by me scooting around the living-dining room. Several days later she changed her mind. A cousin, Muckyi der Royter (the red head) happened to be in the apartment when the order to move the piano was given. Muckyi and my father struggled the piano over the doorsill and began to roll it across the dining room floor. The wheels stuck, caught in bare patches of the linoleum floor covering and tore gashes in it. So, the two men kneeled and lifted the piano to move it. Barely was it off the floor when it toppled and fell with a mighty crash. Every hammer hit every string and the engulfing noise reverberated for a long time.

When they righted the piano half the keys were found to be stuck or mute or producing a shimmering noise not resembling anything known to western music. "Bin eech der nahr udder bist dee?" (Am I the damn fool or

143

are you?) my father asked. "Mirrzennen baydih,"(We're both) said Muckyi, and he left the house.

"Noo, voos yetzt?" (What now?) my mother asked. My father didn't answer. He took his hat and coat and walked out. About ten minutes later he returned.

"Vee bissti gevaysen?" (Where were you?)

"Tzim drugstore barun telephun. Eech hub zay oop-gereefen und gogayben a gooter geshray—'Varrih you min to send me ah brukkin piahnih.' Mittiss tzirick nem-min." (I went to the drugstore and phoned. I yelled real loud: What do you mean to send me a broken piano. They'll take it back.)

Luckily no one was home in the apartment below us when the piano fell. But later that day a very suspicious neighbor came up to find out, "Vee kimmtiss a luch in ceilink bahn intz in hoiz?" (How come there is a hole in our ceiling?) We just didn't know.

That ended piano playing in my family.

The whole incident had an air of unreality. Only two instruments were played on Fox Street—piano and violin. And the sex line was rigidly drawn: boys played violin and girls piano. It was not until I got to high school and played in the school orchestra that I realized that, somewhere, some kids learned to play cello or viola, or woodwinds or brass.

My parents never bought another piano. But my brother and I, in later life, always managed to have a piano in our homes—although neither of us played.

With the piano gone I was constrained, like other little boys, to learn to play the violin. There was a teacher, Mr. Sentner, who gave lessons to several boys on the block. My mother engaged him and bought from him an outfit—complete with a shiny violin, a bow, rosin, pitchpipe and case. He charged 50¢ a lesson. He was well above middle age, wore a grey vest with pearl buttons and piping and wore pince-nez glasses with a heavy black ribbon—the Professor incarnate. He was a terrible teacher. When he set my arms and shoulders in position he made black and blue marks that lasted for weeks. When he tried to illustrate something on the fiddle he would produce ear-piercing scratches.

At the first visit, having twisted me into position with the fiddle under my chin and the bow in my hand, he had me draw the bow on the string and called my mother to listen. With finger pointing to the ceiling he declaimed. "De boy vill be a meister!" Part of his act.

I did not last long with Mr. Sentner. He was bad and I was worse. I neglected practice and took the fiddle in hand only after my mother banged repeatedly into my ear, "Natie, prectice!" While I was practicing she would shout, from the sink or the stove, "Nitt reechtig!" (Not right!) All very discouraging.

My determination to be rid of Mr. Sentner was stronger than my mother's willingness to keep spending 50¢ a week for lessons for a kid that used every known excuse to avoid practicing. And so Mr. Sentner exited from my life.

I would have given up the fiddle for good at this point, as most kids did, except for Lev Rosen. Lev was a few years older than I. Although he lived near us I knew him first from his father's music store on Westchester Avenue, where I bought strings. Sometimes, when I was in the shop, I would hear violin playing from behind the curtain that separated the store front and back. I would stand, transfixed. It was clear, clean, forceful and compelling. Runs and arpeggios were fluently accomplished, double-stops up and down the scale; marvelous.

Mr. Rosen, Lev's father, stood at the counter, watching me. He nodded toward the back and said proudly, "Vundirfool, hah? Dot's my son, Levallih. *Diss* is a violin*ist!*"

In other visits I met Lev at the store. He played for me, or let me come to the back to listen while he practiced. He was, he said, in a matter-of-fact way, going to have a concert career after he completed his studies at a Conservatory in Budapest.

Lev was single minded, dull and indifferent to anything but his music. He was a driven boy. Once I saw him walk down Fox Street with his father. Mr. Rosen had a length of broomstick in his hand and, as they walked, he would strike at an iron fence railing or a garbage can and ask, "Noo, Levallih?" And the boy would say, "Between f sharp and g."

I was bitten by the ambition to become as accomplished a fiddler as Lev Rosen. And so, without any further prompting from my mother I found ways of struggling along with the violin. Before going further I should say that years later, while sitting in one of the front rows of a burlesque theatre I saw Lev Rosen in the pit—a worn looking man, young as he was, pulling wearily at "A Pretty Girl is Like a Melody."

While still gnawed by envy of Lev Rosen I saw an ad for "New York Music School—banjo, ukulele, guitar, accordion, violin and piano. Personal attention, 25¢ a lesson," The school was on 14th Street near Lüchows restaurant, in a walk-up. I went. My teacher was an adenoidal, limp young man. The lessons were supposed to last a half hour. By the time the money was paid, the bow rosined, the fiddle tuned and the music set up, fifteen minutes went by. From then on the lesson was my pushing and pulling the bow across the strings with the teacher behind me, reading a book and saying occasionally, "Do it again," or "Good," until the time was up. Then he became alert, hustled me off and went back to his book, or to the next victim.

My next teacher was Mr. Millacomte. He was a pleasant and agreeable man and a competent fiddler. He was also a serious teacher—charging a dollar a lesson. He lived in a ground floor apartment, a trolley ride and a good walk away from Fox Street. He was short, olive skinned and had long smooth black hair. He had, lying about, programs of his last student concert, somewhere in Yonkers. I read the blurb. It went something like this: "Amadeo Millacomte's youth in Genoa was spent next to the famous brick works where modeling clay was plentiful. His early experience with modeling clay gave him a rich sense of the plastic possibilities of tonal shapes—a belief which infuses his approach to playing and teaching…"

I would listen to Mr. Millacomte's playing, straining to hear some plastic possibilities of tonal shapes. All I heard was pleasant notes. Later I surmised that Mrs. Millacomte had written the blurb.

She was a multiple surprise. I knew her first as a telephone voice. If I called to change or cancel a lesson she would answer, with the rising inflection of a phone company

147

operator, "Oh! Ah-mah-dee-oh will be disappointed!" or, "Tuesday at five? Let me check the shed'ule here. M…m…m Yes! Tuesday is just fine!"

When I first met her I blinked. She was a full head taller than Mr. Millacomte, obviously of Scandinavian stock, broad, blonde, blue-eyed and fair-skinned. She treated him as she would a pet puppy. As I got to know them a little better I observed that this doting was sometimes too much for him. She once looked down at me, with her hands clasped and said, "Ah-mahdeeoh is *so* proud of your progress!" He, standing by growled, "Amadayoh would be more proud to go on with the lesson!" After she left he shook his head. "Sometimes she's a lot to take. But she cooks up a wonderful spaghetti."

Mr. Millacomte thought I should study the violin seriously. He was being considered for a position in a European conservatory and, if I accompanied him, he would see to it that no tuition would be needed.

I pleaded at home to be allowed to go. My father merely shrugged.

"Ah moozicahnt? Sizza schvair laben!" (It's tough to be a musician!) My mother was adamant. "Eech hub deer nit gekoyft a feedle fin deer tzoo machen ah Mischa Elman!" (I didn't buy you a fiddle to make a Mischa Elman out of you!) Sic transitted Millacomte.

Public (Elementary) School

Public school was the least important part of my education. P.S. 52 on Kelly Street was a drab, brick prison ruled by a fat, red-faced domineering boss janitor, the superintendent, named Mr. McKeever. This brute rarely spoke to a kid without batting him on the ear so hard that the kid (including myself) heard bells in his head and was glassy-eyed for hours after. This was sometimes done in the presence of the Principal, Mr. McCarthy, a small, thin, acidic Irishman who would smile approvingly. They were fear-making, hateful people. In the early years I was merely afraid of them. As I progressed through the grades I came to believe that they shared in common a) a hatred of Jewish kids and b) graft from the vendors of school supplies.

Equally memorable were some of the teachers: The arithmetic teacher, a flat-faced, pockmarked, brusque woman who obviously hated the world and children in particular. She raced through lessons, treated questions in a way that showed contempt for the questioner's ignorance and strangled any hope (small indeed it would be) that arithmetic would ever have any charm for me. There was Miss Doyle, a tall woman with extremely broad hips and a narrow chest, a long face made even longer by a coiled bun rising like a loaf at the top of her head. She always wore black skirts and white blouses and, in the pantheon of my memories, stands out because she insisted that we rest our hands on a separate sheet of paper when writing because, "The cleanest hand in the country sweats." She uttered also the dictum that "Men's voices are so much more beautiful than women's!"

Then there was Miss Schwartz—a soft-eyed, gentle woman whom we all loved. We decided once to "follow her home." She lived not very far from the school and, as she started up the steps of her apartment house, turned to us (who were surprised that she knew we were there) and said, "That is not a nice thing to do."

I have here written a lie. In fact one of us (and I think it was I) stamped and shuffled to attract her attention as she was entering her building.

How ashamed and embarrassed we were!

Few indeed were those in charge of us at P.S. 52 who evoked any affection from us. I went through the school for most of the time huddled in my shell, feeling no kinship or contact with the teachers, serving my enforced time in a foreign, inimical world. Yet those were the days in which a "titschirr" stood close to God; when a parent, summoned to be lectured about an unruly kid, trembled as much as the kid; when, in any dispute between school authority and a child, the guilt and the sin were automatically the child's.

The real schools were the tailor shop, the grocery, the basement of the Synagogue and the waste stretches of Springhurst between Southern Boulevard and the East River.

The Tailor Shop

To the needle-trade workers on the block, Mr. Krumweg's tailor shop was the Fox Street equivalent of the small town store with the potbelly stove. The steam presser which exuded lovely warm jets of steam on cold nights was the equivalent of the stove. Here, in the evenings, they gathered to play pinochle, gossip and argue—mostly argue. They were men of every political and personal stripe. They were vocal and passionate about the issues that then stormed through the uneess (unions).

Here I heard the hyphenated epithets hurled in a rich combination of Yiddish and what passed as English:

"Ah-toochis-lecker (ass-licker)—tool fin dih bussess," "Ah crookey labor-faker sussialist-fahrfeerer (misleader)"; the expostulations of those who believed that unions should have political identity and those who believed that they should not; of the "intellactchils" who could see arguments on both sides; of the committed communists, whom the others accused of wanting to wreck any union they could not control; of the men who listened quietly until they burst, "Zite schoyn shtill," "Ginnig shoyn," "Klupt eych baydih dih kepp in vahnt," "Udder schpeelt min coorrtin udder nit!" (Be quite already, enough already, go both of you and knock your heads against the wall, do we play cards or don't we!)

And the rhetoric: thrust and evasive parry—"Only ah schloomp would make ah ahgumint like diss!" "Who you cullink ah schloomp?" "Did I say you are ah schloomp?" The ricochet—"Ah'm *tahlink* you!" "*You* tahlink *me?*" "*Ah'm* tahlink *you!*" The velvet punch—"How could ah men wit your saychil (good sense) believe sahtsh a bunch dreck (shit)?"

Mr. Marshall's Grocery

Rarely was a dozen eggs or a loaf of bread traded without a discussion. From an inflation-angered customer: "Vee woik. Vee are sqveezed ahlt (out) and trewn in de gobbidge pail!" I thought about this when I heard it and said: "Suppose everybody owned stock in the companies. Wouldn't everybody share the profits?" From Mr. Marshall: "A kligger yingle!" (A smart kid!) From the customer, "Zoll ehr vissin fin tsooris vie er vayst voos titsach in der velt." (May he know as little of sorrow as he knows what's doing in the world.)

In fact a trip back to the house—less than fifty feet—from Marshall's grocery from an errand to buy a quart of milk was one of the pivotal points in my life. It was a burning hot day. I had just left the store—shady, cool and smelling slightly of butter and cheese. I sat on the curb with my feet on the asphalt and sipped from the small pail into which Mr. Marshall had just ladled the cool milk. In front of me on the asphalt was a torn piece of newspaper. It was a piece of the editorial page of the *World*. On the scrap was part of a cartoon showing a small man reaching toward a basket of food hanging far above his head from a rope stretched over a pulley. Someone on the other side was pulling the rope. The small man had a tag attached to him: "Consumer." I read it as "consummer" and thought it to be another word for "customer." The basket rising beyond his reach was tagged "cost of living." But the scrap was torn so that I could not tell who it was, on the other side of the pulley that was raising the cost of living basket beyond the consumer's reach. I wondered about that while I was sipping the milk. Before I knew it I had emptied the pail. I never found out who the guilty one was on the other side. And for years my interest in economics, history, law and finance was spurred by my urge to find out. To no avail.

The Walk to Barretto Point

One block east of Fox Street was Southern Boulevard, with the trolleys that ran open during the summer. Beyond that was Whitlock Avenue.

Beyond that ran the New Haven tracks, crossed by iron bridges which, even then, were rusty and rickety. The bridge that we used to cross the tracks was the scene of a crap game that recurred every Friday evening. Railroad workers with their pay in their pockets, the Riordan boys from my tenement, Sammy Raden and others would play. The stakes were high. Mostly I watched. Once, with some change in my pocket (I had been paid at an afternoon job) I threw down a quarter to "fade" (cover the roller's bet) along with the others. The roller crapped. I had fifty cents. I faded him—with fifty cents. He rolled a point and then hit seven. I had a dollar. I faded the next roller and the next and the next, never touching the dice. Soon I was holding a bundle of bills in my hand and had a heavy load of change in my pocket.

Someone must have gone back to Fox Street and told my mother I was shooting crap. She came after me, saw me with the money in my hand, yanked me away by the collar and yelled, pulling the bills from my hand, "Doos iz trayfene gelt—usst rnehr?" (This is unclean money—is that all you have?) My pockets were emptied—crap winnings, my week's pay—all. I never saw a penny of it.

Beyond the bridge were stretches of sparsely inhabited lots and deserted farmland, pavement for streets that began and ended nowhere, being slowly eroded and covered with weeds. Small factories, isolated tenements standing out like lonesome sentinels surrounded by wastes. Part of this walk threaded through dumps in which litter from piano factories, metal stamping shops, demolished houses, fire-damaged goods, etc. were strewn. Sometimes the object of a walk was to retrieve goodies from the dumps. (For some reason we used the word "bunk" to describe a rich source of a goodie. "I found a rope bunk—or a lollypop stick bunk," etc.) Sometimes it was to get to Barretto Point (B.A.B.—bare-ass-beach) for a swim in the East River.

Almost always we took these walks in groups. This was, in part, for protection. We were in a foreign country. This was Springhurst and was populated with the Jew-hating Irish kids who would make raids on Fox Street and, in their own territory, attack any of us or any group of us they thought they could beat up. A Springhurst raid into our territory was an unforgettable experience. They came armed: bats, broken bottles, lengths of BX cable with vicious sharp claws projecting from the ends of the coiled flexible metal. We kids responded as suited our nature. Some of us just fled to our apartments and hid (as I did, mostly). Others grabbed rocks, bottles, garbage pails, and scooted up to the roofs, from which they could counter attack. Some few stood ground and fought. Once, in utter contradiction to my natural cowardice, I stood and fought. We had been playing one-a-cat. I was up and had a three-foot length of broom handle with me. I was attacked by a Springhurst kid with a four-foot length of BX cable. One of my parries was unsuccessful. I still have the long white scar on my right forearm from the rip of the BX claw.

Sometimes I would walk by myself across the bridge into the Springhurst wastes. Not really by myself; a black dog that slept in front of one of the garages on 156th across from Southern Boulevard would almost always struggle up from his snooze, wag his tail and walk with me—usually far ahead. I would walk slowly, kick up dust in the dry paths, study the weeds, crouch to watch ant mounds, pick up and inspect strange machine parts, catch grasshoppers and let them exude their brown juice on my thumbnail.

On one of these walks I was attacked by three Springhurst kids who knocked me down and, in response to the suggestion of one of them: "Let's cockilize him!" pulled down my pants, stuffed rough excelsior against my genitals and groin and rubbed it against my skin, sat on my chest and legs and threatened to knock my teeth out if I didn't get up, kneel and say, "I'm a fuckin' sheeny and Jesus Christ is my master!" I did this and was let go. I am missing an essential ingredient of human nature. Neither then nor since did this experience generate in me any prejudice.

Those kids were hateful and I still think so. But what they did produced no reverberation of anti-Catholic or anti-Irish in me.

The Basement of the Synagogue

I went to Chayder (Hebrew School) intermittently from the age of eight until I was ready to prepare for my Bar Mitzvah. I never learned so little anywhere as I did at Hebrew School or during my Bar Mitzvah preparation. During that preparation something in me rebelled. Chayder is a blurred memory of badly lit class rooms, noisy kids and short tempered teachers, pictures of Theodore Herzl (founder of Zionism), white and blue flags with the Star of David in the center—the Jewish national flag, learning the Jewish national anthem, parading around the room waving little flags.

My keenest memories of class at Chayder are a pair of related incidents. In a Hebrew text I came across the word "oo-fuck-tay-noo." With angelic face I asked the teacher what it meant. He was constrained to repress his rage and answer—something utterly innocent. Not long after, I made recompense for this piece of naughtiness. The teacher was translating a text from the Hebrew and was stumped by a word. He knew what it meant, but lacked an English equivalent. "How," he asked, "do you call a hair-color vich is brahn but vitt sahm rahd in it?" I piped up, "Auburn." He paused for a moment and then nodded. "Ubboin! Yeah. Ubboin." The word pleased him. For the rest of the translation he stressed the word whenever it appeared: "Ubboin!"

The response to my overt break with Chayder was mild. From my mother: "Denk nawr vifill gelt mir hub-ben shoyn bahtzoolt fahr'n Chayder." (Think how much we've already spent on the Chayder.) From my father: "Vill er nit, vill er nit. Verr sih vill nit ken min nit machen a yeed." (If he doesn't want, he doesn't want. You can't make a Jew of someone who doesn't want.) In contrast to my mother, he accepted and liked the shicksih (gentile girl) I married. He had only one request: if we had boy children to have them circumcised.

Hebrew school was in the late afternoon. One evening a week, in a basement room, a group of men would meet. They were the Chevreh Mishnaies (the companions of the law). Mostly older men with beards, some clean shaven, sitting around a table, large books of commentaries open in front of them, their yarmilkis (skull caps) bobbing as they read and talked. In Yiddish they would propound le-gal problems to each other and expound on the reasoning given by the great commentators. "If a seller sells a cow with only one good eye, not knowing of the defect and the buyer, after bringing the cow home discovers it, what is the seller's obligation? Does his innocence make any difference? If one walks on the way with a long pole on his shoulder and another walks before him with a jar of oil on his shoulder and stops abruptly and unexpectedly so that the one with the pole cannot stop himself in time, and breaks the jar, what is his liability? Is there any liability for the spilling of oil on the clothes?" And so on—laws of marriage, laws of master and servant, etc.

How I listened, rubbing the snot from my nose with my sleeve and pulling up long stockings that were constantly working their way down from my knickers. I was hearing law as a pure exercise in right and wrong—a taste rarely gratified in my relations with clients.

THE WAY UP AND OUT

If it is true that Jews have respect for learning, it is a truth that can be known only of those with whom one is intimate.

My father and mother knew enough Hebrew to say (as they almost never did) the prayers contained in the Siddur. My mother claimed to be a lady lahmdin (scholar). I never saw proof of it. Neither ever opened a book. The reading of both was limited to *Der Toog* (The Day) a politically innocuous Jewish daily, and to a section called "Tschikovih Nyess" (unusual news). Credulously they would read about the fish monger in Chlotz who found his mother's lost wedding ring in a fish's stomach; or about the lady in Peoria who willed a million dollars to her cat; or about the man who shot himself in the head and lived another forty years with the bullet in his brain and with no worse damage than being unable to remember names beginning with vowels.

Thoroughly Jewish as they were, they were also naturally secular (without being anti-religious). They were indifferent to politics. They went sometimes to the theatre, if a great name like Maurice Schwartz or Molly Picon played at a Bronx house. But they could take or leave it.

Yet the education of their sons was vital to them. As to my sister, the oldest of the children, she was female, destined to work until she married. When my mother's conception of a desirable husband appeared—tall, born in this country and having a job, my sister's marriage was hastened and blessed. She never forgave my mother for not helping and encouraging her to educate herself.

The next younger was a brother. He was too old when he came to this country to begin school at the beginning and old enough to have his own will. He chose to be a plumber, worked as an apprentice and in the evenings went to the Baron de Hirsch School to learn the trade thoroughly. He did his homework faithfully—spent night after night reading or wiping joints (dripping melted solder over a pipe joint and swiping it around with a canvas pad so that a neat bulge was made, evenly around the joint, smooth, strong and watertight).

My mother could not, with all her force and driving will, get him to take general academic subjects. He foiled her by marrying and becoming a father early. But she fought for second best. Married or not, he had to find his way out of overalls. She brought to bear on him the full array of her considerable talents. She covered him like a tent caterpillar and hung on like a bull terrier. She persisted until he studied something—at first, cost estimating for the building trades, then real estate. His escape from overalls was into a real estate office in Queens—then bouncing with building and land trading activity. He worked as a salesman at first. Soon he formed a partnership with a slick-talking fellow named Polly (born Polykronakos). With money that my mother literally tore from my father's hands, or stole from his pockets and from his cash registers, and hoarded, she helped my brother to support himself while his business was building.

Soon he shed this partner, and others, and began to take courses in insurance. As the real estate business tapered down and the insurance business grew he finally prospered. But whether or not he prospered was not as important to my mother as that he wore business suits, had clean hands and often sat at a desk. He never lost his love for plumbing and at the least excuse would take a wrench in his hand or give his advice.

The next younger brother had formed an ambition to be a doctor even before he came to this country at the age of nine. One of the odd jobs he did as a child in Czernowitz was to collect bones for a woman who burned them to produce bone black. He would wander through the streets picking through garbage for bones and carry them in a sack to the bone blacker. On his route he passed a doctor's house—a low brick structure with casement windows. It had a neatly trimmed lawn strewn with gaily colored outdoor toys and was bordered by a high iron fence and dense, sculptured privet. He would stop and look at the place for a time, and then shuffle away with his sack of bones.

I know, intimately, what that house looked like— even though this passage in my brother's life preceded my birth. I know because the kid with the bone sack formed an ambition: to become a doctor and build a house exactly like that one. He did both.

This brother never had to be pressed to go to school—except once, after his graduation from Columbia College (where his tuition had been financed in part by the family, in part by loans and scholarships and in part by earnings from the operation of a dormitory laundry collection and delivery service). During the summer following graduation he operated a lucrative dairy route in Rockaway. There he met his wife-to-be, a schoolteacher, whose parents owned a Tudor style summerhouse with a tennis court. Money and marriage were uppermost in his mind. He neglected to apply to medical schools for admission. When he told this to my mother she slapped her cheeks, rocked from side to side and keened, moaned and cried in a grief that could not be matched if she had learned that he committed suicide.

For the next few days the life of all of us at home was a hell. My brother's expostulations were in vain: it was too late; they don't take Jews anyway; he could make money in butter and eggs and marry a teacher. The moaning and wailing continued.

A few days later there occurred an event which, to this day, baffles and awes my brother and me. My mother, calm and serene, told my brother that she had had a dream. In it my brother went to see the Dean of the Columbia medical school—P&S. She dreamed that the Dean greeted my brother, asked him to sit down and offered him a glass of wine. My brother asked whether it would be possible to enter the medical school in a late admission. The Dean asked for his college record and after looking through it shook hands with my brother and told him he could enroll.

My brother saw the "dream" as one of her tricks. But he was persuaded to yield to her insistence that he visit the Dean of P&S by her promise (which wasn't really worth two cents) that if he failed to be admitted she would stop badgering him.

He went. He came back stunned. It had happened just as my mother had dreamed—the wine, the reading

162

of the college record, the handshake, the admission. My mother had often before claimed visionary and clairvoyant powers and we had scoffed at her.

What led my parents, who lived a meager life, to make these sacrifices for their children? I think their motives differed somewhat. My father, I believe, wished his sons to be free from subjection to a boss and equally free of dependence on others in doing one's work and making one's way. Success in business of any kind would be difficult without either or both. The obvious way up and out was through a profession.

My mother's motives were, I think, revealed by a small incident. She had once gone to the office of a utility company to pay a bill. She was starry-eyed when she came home. In Yiddish she mooned: "Such a big place, filled with all those clean people, with suits and ties and eye-glasses. They sit at a desk and they write on paper. It is so light and quiet. Only the typewriter machines make such a nice sound."

This was the paradise of security and orderliness and respectability. And these were what she wanted for her children. She knew of no way it could be gotten, except through education.

How different were these views from those associated with learning among the pious Jews in the ghettos of Europe. There, a young man who was a fool could earn great respect and be sought after as a son-in-law if he knew the Siddur (prayer book) by heart, was able to quote liberally from the Torah and able to stick a pin into Talmud text and know every word pierced by the pin in the pages following.

Respect for such learning is a fool's respect for an idiot savant. There were wise men among the learned—the storehouse of Jewish folk tales is filled with instances of this wisdom. But it was wisdom despite learning and not because of it.

I have a nostalgia for lost aspects of Jewish life. But not for the pungent insularities of the ghettos—including learning. Mine is for the Fox Streets, now gone, burned out, lying in rubble, where a kid could once yell up, "Ma! Varrf meer aroonter a schtickle broyt'n pitter." (Ma! Throw me down a little piece of bread and butter.)